MORE ADVANCE PRAISE FOR

TRUE STYLE

"The Ivy Style exhibition at The Museum of the Fashion Institute of Technology in New York City, for which Mr. G. Bruce Boyer was a consulting curator, is still being talked about among fashion leaders in Japan. We respect Mr. Boyer, whose appraisal of Ivy Style always influences new fashion trends worldwide."

—Minoru Onozato, editor-in-chief,
***Free & Easy* magazine**

"*True Style* combines historical insight, an elegant turn of phrase and sartorial authority, all enhanced with timeless illustrations. It is the perfect complement to the connoisseur's wardrobe and bookshelf."

—Christopher Breward,
University of Edinburgh

"*True Style* is magic. G. Bruce Boyer's delightful writing gives us a chance to contemplate the beauty and function of men's wardrobe essentials, transporting us to a world where old-world glamour and modern elegance rule. With rich erudition, Boyer brings together dress history, fashion pedagogy, smart anecdotes, and examples of timeless style icons to show how the art and pleasure of male dressing can be mastered."

—Masafumi Monden, author of *Japanese Fashion Cultures:*
Dress and Gender in Contemporary Japan

TRUE STYLE

G. BRUCE BOYER

TRUE STYLE

The HISTORY *&* PRINCIPLES
of CLASSIC MENSWEAR

BASIC BOOKS
A Member of the Perseus Books Group
New York

Designed by Cynthia Young

Library of Congress Cataloging-in-Publication Data
Boyer, G. Bruce.
True style : the history and principles of classic menswear / G. Bruce Boyer.
pages cm
Includes bibliographical references and index.
ISBN 978-0-465-05399-5 (hardback)—ISBN 978-0-465-06159-4 (e-book)
1. Men's clothing.   2. Grooming for men. I. Title.
TT618.B69 2015
646.4'02—dc23
2015019125

10 9 8 7 6 5 4 3 2 1

For Pam

CONTENTS

INTRODUCTION

"You appear to read a good deal upon her which was quite invisible to me," I remarked.

"Not invisible, but unnoticed, Watson. You did not know where to look, and so you missed all that was important. I can never bring you to realize the importance of sleeves, the suggestiveness of thumb-nails, or the great issues that may hang from a boot-lace."

—SIR ARTHUR CONAN DOYLE, "A CASE OF IDENTITY"

Exactly—the great issues that may hang from a boot lace! How many times have our parents and teachers said much the same thing, admonishing us that prospective employers surreptitiously note the condition of our nails and shoes, and can read therein our whole character? Human resources directors, we've been led to imagine, must be trained by the FBI.

But of course it's not just potential employers who notice such things. Parents and teachers obviously do. So too do actual employers and colleagues; lovers, friends, and acquaintances; and—perhaps most importantly—*prospective* lovers, friends, and acquaintances. Who among us has not scoffed at the ill-fitting suit of a stranger or stolen a disdainful glance at their coworker's frayed slacks? Who has not judged a date by the clothes he or she was wearing? Do we assume others don't do the same?

Conan Doyle knew what he was talking about: it's the little things, the subtleties and miniscule details in the clothes you wear, that say the most. Is your hosiery over your calves, for instance, or do your socks sag down around your ankles, making your shins look like plucked chickens' necks? Is your tie discreet or garish? And what about the pocket handkerchief—the one for show, not for blow? Does it accentuate or clash with your shirt and tie? Is it even there at all?

Let's, for the moment, forgo the moral question about whether these matters of dress and grooming, of posture and manner *should* matter, because the reality is that they do. We must leave it to others to determine whether Oscar Wilde was right or wrong when he suggested that it's only shallow people who don't judge by appearances. Suffice to say that comportment and appearance are noticed—and that they speak volumes about us.

As Sherlock Holmes noted, the accessories that support the tailored wardrobe are of particular importance as personal and social indicators precisely because they tend to have no other real function, no utilitarian purpose, and are otherwise completely unnecessary except as symbols of status and clues to aspirations. Historically, jewelry is an obvious indicator of status for both men and women, but for the modern man—at least, the modern man with a sense of taste and decorum—there are more subtle signs than large chunks of gold around the wrist or dangling from the sternum.

I never tire of saying—readers might, but I don't—that clothes speak. In fact they never shut up. And the great danger is that if you don't hear them, you're not listening closely enough and will have to pay whatever penalty accrues from such inattention. As the English statesman Lord Chesterfield pointed out, dress is a foolish thing, and yet it's a more foolish thing not to pay attention to it.

Not only do clothes speak, but they also lie less than words do. We know that most communication is nonverbal, and much of that is based solely on visual clues we gather from each other.

In today's world, when our quick meetings, fast meals, and ubiquitous technology have wedged a larger and larger space between us, we are forced to make decisions in nano-seconds and get our evidence wherever we can. Much of our evidence comes from our visual perceptions, from what we see. And what both individuals and society as a whole see is fashion. And because clothes speak, it follows that they constitute a sort of grammar—a set of rules that channel the vast possibilities of the language into meaningful, intelligible messages. Yet somehow, despite the obviousness of clothing as a tool of communication, we tend to take its grammar for granted—or even to deny its very existence.

I know most people don't read trade fashion magazines or blogs. I don't read them much myself with the zealousness I should. I suppose I'm afraid they'll do something terrible to my brain pan. But I did pick up a magazine the other day, on the assumption that I'd learn a bit from the lead article, entitled "New World Order." I stopped reading after the first sentence: "The new rule of dressing for the workplace is that there are no rules." It brought tears to my eyes. Of laughter.

Of rules there are no end, for fashion or anything else. It's simply that they change from time to time, sometimes slowly, sometimes with a quickness and ferocity unimaginable: whole empires gone in the blink of an eye. You may have noticed that, one recent summer, every man in the world seemed to be paring a navy blazer with white jeans. Very natty of course, but en masse you felt like the streets were populated by the chorus from Gilbert and Sullivan's *H.M.S. Pinafore*. I mean, fair enough, it's a chic look, but after you've seen thirty or forty men on the street wearing the Look, it gets a bit, well, boring. It's not that there's anything intrinsically wrong with a uniform; it's just that it can become such a cliché, revealing little more than that the man wearing it is achingly up to date and running hard with the pack.

Fashion goes back and forth, reacting more violently against itself than Newton's third law would seem to allow for a purely physical object. But that's the modus operandi of fashion, isn't it—to move antithetically, almost Hegelian in its constant vacillation between seemingly opposing extremes? One season it's all skinny gray mohair; the next it's oversized tweed. As the times change, the man in the gray flannel suit becomes the peacock revolution, Milanese chic, the vintage revival, *la mode* preppy, or romantic rebellion. It never makes much sense except at the moment.

The goal of this book is to help you transcend the moment—to describe a set of items, styles, and traditions that are at once rooted in history and possessed of a timeless elegance that will see you through the next five seasons, or the next fifty. The objective is to help you achieve rational elegance, if I may put it that way, by means of a constant dialogue between innovation, tradition, and individual taste.

The style of dress described in these pages is historically Western in origin, particularly British in the last three centuries and more, but the fact that it has endured for several hundred years now and spread around the globe is some testament to its worth. The begnnings of the three-piece suit were in the middle of the seventeenth century, but later generations of popular costume and fashion writers—the James Lavers and Pearl Binders, the Cecil and Phillis Cunningtons, the Christopher Brewards and Peter McNeils of this small world—would notice a decided sartorial shift for men occurring rather briskly by the turn of the nineteenth century.

We now refer to this moment as the Great Renunciation, a movement away from gorgeousness and toward simplicity. In the first several decades of the century, men gave up silks and satins, embroidered coats and powdered wigs and silver-buckled shoes in favor of woolen suits simply cut and soberly colored. In other words, men doffed what we might call court dress and donned the modern suit.

Before the Great Renunciation, menswear was a wholly different beast from what it is today. Embroidered silk, satin, and velvet predominated among European elites through the first half of the eighteenth century, until two revolutions with tremendous and unforeseen implications determined what people would wear for the following two centuries and more. The French Revolution, striking a great blow against the silk and satins of court dress, and the following Industrial Revolution, both coming at the end of the eighteenth century, constituted a true watershed in human events, not the least in people's appearance.

Toward the close of the eighteenth century, Europeans began adopting a new mode of dress—one whose ties to liberal democracy during the intervening years have only strengthened. The fading century, in the words of historian David Kuchta, created a "self-confident capitalist class, having expelled an old regime driven by court-sponsored conspicuous consumption and replaced it with an economic culture based on masculine conceptions of industry and frugality." A rising urban, professional, business, and manufacturing class found no practicality in satin breeches and silver-buckled shoes and powdered wigs, and eventually sensed that there was not even any symbolic worth in such things, either.

George "Beau" Brummell stands as a synecdoche for this shift, and much credit has been given him ever since for advancing the standard outfit of the business class: plain wool coat and trousers, white linen shirt, and necktie. Brummell's great contribution to social history is that he made style a criterion for advancement, while theretofore it had been bloodlines; in sartorial history, he brushed away the trappings of courtier dress—the jeweled waistcoats and perukes and velvet breeches—and replaced them with a version of the well-to-do squire's fox-hunting kit. Simplicity, utility, and cleanliness were his goals, and in this sense he was a product of his time, which—like ours—was defined by the popular advancement of representative democracy, the rise of large urban centers, the industrial and technological revolutions, mass manufacturing and media, a higher standard of living through science, and a bureaucratic corporate class.

As with these other aspects of Brummell's age, what changes have occurred in dress since his lifetime are matters of degree, rather than kind. He is credited, rightly, with creating the first modern urban uniform. It was minimalist; it was revolutionary. We wear it still.

Brummell's own life turned sour and went downhill fairly early on, but his ideas about a gentleman's dress and grooming have endured. True, the business suit has gone through succeeding evolutions since Brummell's day, but it's been relatively unchanged in over a hundred years now. His daywear outfit was not dissimilar to our own blue blazer–odd trouser outfit: blue wool tailcoat, plain vest, buff-colored trousers, white shirt, and muslin neckwear. No powdered wigs or fancy embroidery or silver buckles. In the evening he wore black and white. And even more remarkably for the times, he bathed and changed clothes daily. His biographer Captain Jesse noted that Brummell early on "shunned all external peculiarity, and trusted alone to that ease and grace of manner which he possessed in a remarkable degree. His chief aim was to avoid anything marked, one of his aphorisms being that the severest mortification a gentleman could incur was to attract observation in the street by his outward appearance."

Those are the bare bones of the story anyway, and contemporary fashion historians have found much on which to elaborate and debate about this Age of Corporate Man. But if we have indeed foregone the gorgeousness of dress in the eighteenth century—still enjoyed by women to some extent—can't we find a bit of individuality and color somewhere in the tailored wardrobe? Must we continue to suppress our poetic souls and hide our light under a bushel of dreary worsted? What really are our options? That's where I'd like to direct the discussion.

Ironically, men's sartorial choices have become all the more defining as their wardrobe choices have become more limited. In the first half of the nineteenth century, as the great European metropolises expanded and more and more people crowded into larger and larger cities, appearances became homogenized, less idiosyncratic and local. A subtle process of decoding evolved. With the rise of the middle class, symbolism in dress became more subtle. Dress became a matter of "taste" rather than blatant show. The task of differentiating the gentleman from the poseur (when, and if, such a difference existed at all) accordingly became an intricate game of discrimination and acute discernment that remains with us today.

This competition between the aficionado and the sham is not just a matter of finery; there were, and are, artful rules of engagement. It's usually thought that gentlemen's dress rules reached their apex in the English Edwardian era, when male members of society would change complete outfits half a dozen times a day depending on the time, company, and occasion. Under such duress, as you can well imagine, the anxiety about proper dress was extremely high, caused, it is usually thought, by the flux and increasing instability of the social categories. One didn't want to find oneself perceived as a member of the lower ranks of society, lest those appearances become reality. Personal taste didn't really enter into it except in the minutest of detail. Just because you fancied something wasn't a good enough reason to wear it and possibly risk your station in life as a result.

As it happens, anxiety levels regarding fashion seem rather high today too, if you consider that sartorial blogs are awash with blueprints for tastefully correct dress, often accompanied by photos to illustrate the proper assemblage. These sites will undoubtedly provide reams of evidence for fascinating future sociological study; for the moment, however, they lamentably constitute the most widely available—and for many men, the only—guide for what to wear, how to wear it, and why.

This is sad on a number of levels, but mostly because many men still dress as if they're living in the Edwardian era, rather than taking advantage of the relative freedom modern culture affords us to express ourselves through our clothes. The fact is that well-dressed men are well dressed not because they follow every little rule about clothing, but because they have good taste, individuality, style, and a sense of history. Whether we're talking about the Duke of Windsor and Fred Astaire or Luciano Barbera,

Sean Combs, Jay Z, Nick Foulkes, Ralph Lauren, and George Clooney, the most nattily attired gentlemen have explored pattern, texture, and color combinations in ways that promote a sense of personality, while still being mindful of tradition. Any man, if he takes care, can attain a similar balance.

Each of these men—if I may speak for them—also understands the rules of dressing without getting caught up in the myths. There are so many of the latter, after all, and so many of them make such little sense. This is of course something that fashion magazines usually don't mention: *why* people wear what they wear and, more importantly, why they *don't* wear certain things. I mean, there are good rules when it comes to dress, and then there are all those other rules that get bandied about—you know, about how your pocket handkerchief has to be folded a certain way, and your coat has to be a certain length arrived at by some arcane mathematical formula, and how your trouser cuffs must be a certain width, that sort of thing. And well, let's be honest, so many of them are kind of silly. My motto is, if you like it, wear it. And let the bright tweed deerstalkers, the opera capes, and the spectator shoes fall where they may.

With all of that said, when I talk about "relative freedom" in dress, I mean it. Propriety has its limits, after all, and every man should know them. For instance, there's a large spectrum of casual clothing available to men today. Problem is, one man's casual office attire is another man's workout gear, isn't it? Just because casual dressing is so much a part—perhaps the largest part—of our lives today, is there any reason why it should degenerate into ragged denims, sweatshirts, and running shoes? Just as there are levels of speech, after all, there are levels of dress. And correctness in both would seem to depend on appropriateness: to the purpose, the audience, and the occasion. While a pair of cutoffs may be perfectly appropriate on a deserted beach (as nothing at all might also be), they hardly seem the thing for a cocktail party. But then again, neither do a tie and dress shirt.

Anarchy in dress, we feel, presents problems—as in the aforementioned "no rules" sort of rubbish—which may go way beyond clothing (see the "Broken Window" school of sociology, for example). The unfortunate upshot of the "business casual" thinking awhile back, you may recall, was to eradicate all the outward signs and symbols of rank and seriousness in otherwise serious men. We began to feel, I don't know, just a bit uncomfortable seeing what we thought of as responsible adults dressing like their surf-boarding children. We began asking ourselves, *Do I really want to see my stockbroker or my cardiologist wearing cargo shorts and a T-shirt emblazoned with www.fuckoff.com?* Should I trust my hard-won earnings and future security to an investment adviser who wears those stupidly hyper-designed running shoes and purposefully distressed jeans? Perhaps not.

There's also the problem of the downward spiral. I'll be preparing a full report on this theory for the next meeting of the International Society of the Arts & Sciences, but in the meantime the gist of it is that peer pressure can so often be greater than vanity. We are, after all, pack animals, and a strong tendency to run with the pack is within us all. But when it comes to dress and deportment, that tendency is the desire to be included, rather than to stand out—thus leading to a downward spiral, to refrain from rising above in order to fit in below.

What's a man to do? Go on wearing drab suits for the rest of his life, drowning the very soul of individuality within him in a sea of sludge-colored sack cloth, or slouch about in a hoodie and trainers? Not while there's still a spark of life in him, or while he has the wherewithal to do something about it! Knowing the different options and styles at your disposal, their history and applications, is but the first step in reclaiming your dignity through dress. Every journey, they say, begins with a few small steps. But what sort of shoes to wear once you've started down the road? Let's take the first step together—starting not at the bottom, but rather at the top.

1

ASCOTS

IT IS AN UNFORTUNATE TRUTH that most men have no idea what to do with their necks. When not safely ensnaring their napes in a necktie, they seem to either forego all other options and literally stick their necks out, airing them like so many turkey wattles projecting from their open collars, or attempt solutions with lesser articles of clothing. From time to time, for instance, the turtleneck sweater will make one of its periodic returns to the sartorial scene as a sheath for the exposed gullet, and many—too many—men will embrace it with the passion of the hopelessly desperate. Whole squadrons of otherwise sensible gentlemen will arrive at cocktail parties sporting their navy double-breasted blazers with white turtleneck jerseys. Clustered on the patio, they will resemble nothing so much as a cast of movie extras between takes of *Sink the Bismarck*. (See Chapter 25 for a fuller discussion of the turtleneck.)

There is really no need for all the confusion over the matter of the neck when the perfect solution has for so long been at hand, if you'll pardon that mixed anatomical metaphor: the comfortable, jaunty, and ancient tradition of the scarf. Call it what you will—ascot, cravat, stock—the scarf at the throat is the tested and true answer to the naked neck. It is also the answer for those baffling formal but "dressed-down" occasions when a coat and tie are too stuffy but slacks and a polo shirt are too scruffy. A scarf at the neck provides the right accoutrement to a cashmere cardigan, tweed jacket, navy blazer, or summer sports coat. Nothing so exactly achieves the air of casual elegance, of sporty self-confidence, as a mannerly fold of fine silk or light-weight cashmere with an open collar.

The historical precedent alone would make the case for the cravat, you would think, as the history of neckwear has, in one form or another, been the history of the scarf. When it first crept into existence over four centuries ago, European men had long worn collars around their necks. Think Sir Francis Drake in his ruff collars or the spreading, lace-edged collar that one sees in so many Dutch portraits of the period. By the middle of the seventeenth century, however, a new type of neckcloth began to replace these earlier variants. In imitation of the Dutch collar it was replacing in popularity, it was also lace-edged, so that when wrapped around the neck and tied in front, the lace cascaded down the shirt bosom and gave a handsome touch of decoration when the coat was left open.

Over the years different names have been given to this piece of cloth. The general term up to the nineteenth century was simply "neck-cloth," which could take two different forms: the first, the cravat, was a long strip of cloth wound around the neck and tied in front; the second, the stock, was a band of fabric that passed around the neck and was fastened at the nape with a knot and later a buckle or hook-and-eye arrangement.

At first the cravat held fashionable sway. Some say the idea was first brought to France about 1640 by French officers who had fought beside troops of Croatian mercenaries against the German emperor in the Thirty Years War. These Croats were known to tie their collars together with long flowing strips of cloth, and "cravat" is the French word for Croat. Whatever its origins, this style can be clearly found in paintings after 1650. Worn by monarchs and subjects alike, cravats were either lace-trimmed or, more expensively, all lace and became as popular in America as in Europe. Fine sheer cotton cravats were advertised in the *Boston Evening Post* as early as 1735.

During the first half of the eighteenth century, the popularity of the cravat dipped, and the stock came to dominate neckwear for a time. Its rise is mostly attributed to the increased popularity of the waistcoat, which was tailored to be worn closed from just below the nape to just below the hips, using ten to a dozen buttons, and thus tended to hide the decorative front of the cravat. Ladies and gentlemen of the hunt still wear a modified version of the eighteenth-century stock today. The stock is the only neckwear that is still really functional. It provides protection for the neck—from the sun in the summer and cold in winter—and can be used as an emergency bandage or sling in the field should there be an accident to either rider or horse. Usually made in piqué, linen, silk, or fine cotton, the hunting stock is always white, tied in a prescribed manner, and fastened with a gilt safety pin about three inches long. There's a buttonhole in the middle of the stock, which attaches to a button on the front of the shirt; then the stock is wound front to back, one end is passed through a loop of material on the stock band, then both ends are brought to the front again and tied in a square knot. The pin is used to secure the long ends in front and keep them from flapping in the face. Novice riders like to joke that learning to tie a stock properly is only slightly more difficult than learning to ride.

After 1760 waistcoats came to be worn open again, as a dishabille approach to dress gained popularity for both men and women, and gentlemen of fashion often tied a ruffle of fabric around the stock to flow over the shirt front. This accommodation was called a "jabot." It was in effect a two-piece cravat, and it signaled the demise of the stock.

In the early nineteenth century, the Regency period, the cravat may be said to have come into the full flush of its popularity.

The French Revolution, with its *liberté*, *egalité*, and *fraternité*, had swept away the silk and satin exuberances of the nation's court, and the Industrial Revolution quickly stepped in to replace them with a decidedly more democratic and sober approach. As the great French author Honoré de Balzac pointed out, when the French gained equal rights, they simultaneously acquired sameness of dress. And while there were decreasing differences of style between classes, a gentleman's cravat was a peculiarly telling feature of his wardrobe. Sartorial subtlety was being equated with the democratic spirit. In response to this development, the elegantly tied and starched neckcloth became the hallmark of the true gentleman of refinement. He was called a "dandy"—likely by those who wanted to dress equally lushly but didn't. As consummate followers of fashion, some dandies so voluminously exaggerated their cravats that they rose up over their chins and all but concealed their mouths, which made turning the head a bit tricky and surely helped to confer on the dandy his classic air of imperturbability and hauteur. As the English writer Max Beerbohm explained, the dandy was a painter whose canvas was himself. (It's a noticed curiosity that the dandy's dandy, Beau Brummell, never married, nor seemed to have had a romantic allegiance with anyone, male or female. The great love of his life seems to have been himself.)

Interestingly enough, Balzac himself is the reputed author of an extensive manual on neckwear. (He never acknowledged authorship of the volume, but it is assumed that the name on the cover, H. Le Blanc, is a pseudonym.) The book gives lessons on thirty-two different ways to tie a cravat: a style for every mood and occasion. And lest you think this matter of tying is a minor point: it solidified the legacy of at least one great style icon and social arbiter, George "Beau" Brummell.

Brummell's reputation as a leader of society was in considerable measure based on his finesse with his neckwear. If we are to believe his valet—and why wouldn't we—Brummell spent hours achieving the desired effect with his neckcloth. His friend

George, then the Prince of Wales, sat at his feet to learn the art of tying the linen band with just that proper corrugated dishabille. The prince is said to have been in favor of the large neckband because he suffered from swollen glands, so perhaps he was the one to initially focus public attention on the neckcloth, but Brummell and his dandy friends certainly brought it into prominence as the dandy's imprimatur.

Ian Kelly, in his biography of the Beau, gives the reasons for this. First, the neckcloth was indeed a focal point for the eye and called attention to itself. Second, it became the mark of a gentleman because its scrupulously starched whiteness "gave subtle expression to a disinterest in the cost of linen and laundering." Clean linen signified wealth, status, and thus style for these new men of the Regency. Brummell ensured that the neckcloth would be the symbol of a gentleman's appearance, and it was quite the thing at the time to spend one's entire morning achieving the proper arrangement. There is a story of a visitor calling on Brummell in the middle of the morning and finding him and his valet in his dressing room, knee-deep in discarded cravats. When the visitor inquired what they were, the valet replied, "Oh, sir, those are our failures."

In the mid-nineteenth century the term "necktie" entered the lexicon. By then the cravat had come to be wound around the neck once and tied in front with either a large bow (and thus the "bow tie") or a small knot with long ends left to hang down the shirt front (the predecessor of our contemporary necktie). Neckwear thereafter came to be known by the manner in which it was tied or arranged: the four-in-hand (our contemporary tie, named after the manner in which the reins of a four-horse team are held in the hand), the bow tie (discussed in more detail in Chapter 3), and the famous ascot itself, in which the long blades of the scarf were folded across the shirt front and fixed with a pin—but not, originally, tucked in.

The ascot is, of course, named after the most fashionable event of the London season: the annual race meeting held, as it has been for almost three hundred years now, at Ascot Heath each June. Ascot has always been the dressiest event of the English sporting season, and a broad silk neck scarf fastened with a pin eventually became de rigueur for the occasion. The name took.

It's a shame that the only heartily surviving member of this august triumvirate is the necktie. Why should the others, if you will allow me another mixed metaphor, be endangered species? Why should the bow tie be left to languish around the necks of a few magazine editors, eccentric lawyers, or Ivy League professors? And why should the ascot be proscribed to all but a select natty few and long gone—the Fred Astaires, Cary Grants, and Douglas Fairbankses of the world?

Actually, that, I think, is precisely the rub. The jaunty scarf at the neck has been so associated with aristocratic dress that few men believe they can carry it off well. This casually romantic and slightly flamboyant accessory does not sit easily with some who must dress for their business in a more somber manner, although why an accountant or postal clerk, milkman or bank president should not be accorded the right to a bit of romance and flamboyance I do not understand.

Passion and flair aside, no one has come up with a better method of covering the neck for those occasions when a tie is not wanted. The scarf allows for a tremendous variety in design, color, and style. There are, for example, any number of ways of tying it. In the past ascots were designed in the Edwardian manner, in which the center section—what wound round the neck itself—was a narrow, pleated band, while the blades were considerably wider and often pointed. The idea was that the narrow band around the neck would fit more comfortably under the shirt collar and be less bulky, while the wider blades in front would provide a suitably puffy effect to fill in the shirt opening. This type of ascot is still the one typically sold in menswear shops.

A similar effect, however, can be achieved by other methods. One can use either a square scarf of about thirty-two inches or a long band of about six inches wide and a yard long. The scarf should be folded cornerwise to form a triangle and then rolled apex toward the base until a long band results. In the other case, the band is simply folded until an appropriate width is formed. Both methods are simple and accommodating.

A scarf folded in either of these ways is easy to fix at the front of the neck by any of several different methods. The Duke of Windsor—formerly King Edward VIII and, before that, the Prince of Wales—used to simply and elegantly thread the long ends of the scarf through a finger ring and let them hang down his shirt front. Astaire was known to favor a small tie clip to secure the ends, in the original Ascot fashion. An antique stick-pin, Art Deco jewelry, or perhaps a miniature gold clothespin would all be perfect. On the other hand, simplicity—the greatest of virtues—would recommend a mere knot. Actually, by passing one blade under the knot and then over it, making a flap, it is possible to achieve the appropriate puffiness without the bulk.

There is really no end to the possibilities of the ascot. This is one of those agreeable places where one can indeed be an individual. A man can devise his own way of wearing a scarf, have his own special knot, and make it his signature. There's a chap I know who, when he's not wearing a necktie, always wears a navy-and-white polka-dot scarf, double-knotted. It's his trademark, and it serves and suits him well.

Sometime around the middle of the last century, Brooks Brothers produced one of the simplest solutions to this look: a sports shirt with an attached ascot. The "Brooks-Clarney" shirt (named after the fellow who designed it) was a lovely flannel, checked affair, with an ascot of the same material attached to the neckband, and was perfect for informal entertaining, cocktail parties at the club, and that sort of thing. Unfortunately Brooks has not offered this item for many years, but perhaps if enough interest were shown, it might be revived. The other noteworthy point about this style of neckwear is that it never changes: the same proportions, the same fine silks, even the same classic designs—paisleys, polka dots, geometric prints—have endured across the seasons, so that if you end up buying a new one, it will simply be for color's sake. There is no reason to presume that the ascot will ever be out of fashion.

2

BOOTS

ONCE THE PURELY utilitarian footgear of laborers and out-doorsmen, the boot exploded into the world of fashion around the middle of the last century, and its popularity only continues to grow. Some of the models being offered are new styles, many of them hyper-designed with several materials stitched and glued together to give them a look of super ruggedness worthy of a comic-book hero. And yet every vintage style seems to be available too: authentic versions of work boots, engineer boots, cowboy boots, hiking and field boots, and rubber country boots. There are light-weight trail boots and waterproof hunting boots; heavy-duty, steel-toed construction boots; silicon-treated cowhide or oiled wild boar mechanics' boots; stockmen's riding boots; service boots; Chelsea boots; and gentlemen's country boots in Scotch grain leathers with wing tips and commando soles. Chippewa, Red Wing, Oak Street, Wolverine, Viberg, Russell, L. L. Bean, Wellington, Rider, R. M. Williams, Chamonix, and a dozen others are now familiar names in the retail world, not to mention the country walkers by such renowned firms as Edward Green, Crockett & Jones, Alden, Church's, John Lobb, and others.

Is it because there are many more sportsmen now than a few decades ago? Probably not, although lots more may want to give the impression of the gentrified outdoorsman. But certainly more men find boots a practical alternative to shoes. And many of these styles have a strong and long heritage that is appealing to people today who are interested in the craftsmanship quality and styling of vintage items. Your choice rather depends on whether you intend to merely make a fashion statement, kick around a few leaves in some city park, or exert some serious energy on a marathon hike down the Appalachian Trail. Many of these new sports boots—with their multicolored nylon panels, D-ring lace holes, bumper-styled toe pieces, tank-tread soles, reflective trim, and high-tech breathable membranes—are very comfortable and durable, even if many of them look as though they'd been designed by someone who had read a great deal about boots and shoes but never actually seen any.

Several styles, most of them American in origin, have risen to the top of the list in popularity. The black bull-hide motorcycle boot has been popular with young men ever since the 1950s, when Marlon Brando came roaring into town with a pair in the 1953 film *The Wild One*, and James Dean sauntered around wearing them in *Rebel Without a Cause* two years later. Now they seem to be a strong component of every designer collection, a fashionable nod to a time when style was perhaps more closely attached to utility. There is something almost mythic about these boots, and as art historian Sir Kenneth Clark noted about myths, they don't just die suddenly but go through a period of what he called "respectable retirement" and continue to stoke our imaginations. They become emasculated as they go from original utility to fashion statement.

In designer collections, these prole boots become costume, but there was nothing sleek or aesthete about the originals. Indeed, the boots that accompanied the enormous Harley-Davidson motorcycle became the first really "cool" footwear in this category. The authentic model should strictly speaking be called an *engineer* boot, since it was originally designed for rail-road workers. Chunky and tough, engineer boots were made from thick, stiff bull hide dyed black; the top was not as tight and straightly cut as a cowboy boot, but rather flared upwards with a gusseted top that could be tightened at the ankle by a steel-buckled strap. The vamp ended in a bulbous toe, and the instep had its own steel-buckled strap (sometimes decorated with metal studs). The soles were thick leather, the one-and-three-quarter-inch heel was slanted forwards slightly, and the edges were concave. A shoemaker would nail crescent-shaped metal cleats to the heels. These boots were one rugged type of footwear, weighing in at probably a pound on each foot, and it took a real swagger to wear them. They were the fitting footwear to accompany black leather motorcycle jackets, jeans rolled with high cuffs, form-fitting T-shirts (no logos or messages, please), and greased D.A. ("duck's ass") hairstyles. The total image was the male rebel proletariat as superhero—an archetype that soon ushered in its close relative, the juvenile delinquent, as seen in films such as *Blackboard Jungle*, those featuring Brando and Dean, and a number of other, much less memorable ones today.

Also coming out of the '50s was the work boot: another classic example of modern fashion's tendency to rise from the bottom to the top—not from the top of the social ladder down, as it had always done. This boot, worn mainly in its construction-styled version (i.e., those boots worn by construction workers), was taken up by the so-called Beatniks and other intellectuals in leftist sympathy with the proletariat. Playwrights and poets from Arthur Miller and Allen Ginsberg to Jack Kerouac and Gregory Corso wore the pale-orange leather construction boots with the cream-colored rubber soles and thick laces.

Such prole gear had a laid-back demeanor and working-class appeal for the angry young rebels of the Beat Generation. It was the style of the underclass hero, the prole rebel. The boots were bought in army and navy stores across the United States, along with blue chambray work shirts and khakis, olive-drab T-shirts, leather bomber jackets, and thick garrison belts. The surplus gear was cheap and well-made, and tons of it was available left over from World War II and the Korean War. The look was seen in the aisles of Manhattan's Strand Bookstore and the steps of the Columbia University Library, on the campus of the University of California, Berkeley, and in the coffee shops of Ann Arbor, as well as the clubs of Greenwich Village and bookstores of North Beach, and anywhere else there were youths determined to transcend what they thought were their bland and boring bourgeois lives of stifling conformity by being cool, collected, and loose.

The cowboy boot is yet another reflection of the modern trend for fashion to start low and reach high. Precursors to these high-topped boots were worn by cavalry officers in the US Army even before the Civil War, and the Spanish vaqueros who herded longhorn cattle on the plains north of the Rio Grande had worn boots adorned with metal spurs. As the vaqueros' profession entered the mainstream in America, helped along by many a former US Army officer, so too did these styles of footwear. Particularly after the Civil War, men from the East and South began to drift westward in search of adventure or merely a decent livelihood. A few took jobs tending the huge herds of cattle that grazed the open lands of Texas; these men contributed to the most vibrant, heroic image the United States has ever produced: the American cowboy.

It's worthwhile exploring this iconic figure a bit more, because its influence has been so pervasive in subsequent American history. That colorful period, a mere thirty-odd years, was the time of the "long drives," when thousands of head of Texas longhorns were driven from southern Texas to Wichita and Abilene, Kansas, along the legendary Chisholm Trail so stirringly portrayed in Hollywood epics like *Stagecoach* (John Ford, 1939) and *Red River* (Howard Hawks, 1948). Virtually all of the romantic myths—and the costume—of the cowboy derive from this unique enterprise. Dude ranches became a popular vacation retreat for tourists in the 1930s, but it was the Hollywood cowboy films of the '40s that established a nostalgia for the West of myth and fiction. Particularly influential were the "singing cowboys," those film and recording stars such as Roy Rogers, Gene Autry, Tex Ritter, and Rex Allen who beat up the black-hatted bad guys, kissed the girl, and rode off into the sunset yodeling a song about the beauty of sagebrush. Cowboy hats and fancy boots have been de rigueur for country music stars ever since.

In truth, the life of the long-drive cowboy was lonely and arduous, and his clothes were designed from hard-won experience to provide protection if not solace. His wide-brimmed hat and calico bandana insulated him from scorching sun and choking dust, while tough leather gauntlets and chaps took the beating of horse, rope, and sagebrush. His boots were a special consideration, arguably the most important and expensive facet of his possessions, next to his gun and saddle. By 1800 western cowboy boots had already evolved into what we would consider and recognize as today's model: heels were high (about two inches,

which prevented slipping in the stirrups), tapered, and sharply underslung to dig into the ground as a brace for holding roped cows; arches were high and tight, and toes pointed, which made getting into the stirrups easier and staying there less fatiguing. The upper part of the boot was cut straight just below the knee and made of tough leather to protect the leg from horse sweat, cactus needles, snakebite, flailing cattle hooves, and a dozen other hazards of the range.

In fact, about the only modern element missing from those boots was decoration. By today's standards, they were distinctly unadorned. Exactly when fancy boots started to ride the range or saunter the sidewalks is difficult to say, but the general explanation seems to be that as necessity diminished, sport and entertainment began. With the advent of the railroad, the long drives were no longer necessary, and the cowboys of the Chisholm Trail rode into history, folklore, and legend. But the decline of the long riders marked the beginning of the show biz cowboys. Beginning in the 1880s with Buck Taylor, the first King of the Cowboys, who worked with the Buffalo Bill traveling troupe, and up through the early Western films of William S. Hart, Broncho Billy Anderson, and Tom Mix, the "fancy" cowboy was born. He rode a handsome, well-equipped horse (usually with an endearing name), wore ornate clothes, and a bit later played a decorated guitar and crooned to a wholesome lass of impeccable virtue. In his world the only unadorned element was his moral code: he hated bad men and injustice and knew exactly what to do when he found them.

American actor Tom Mix was the first to portray the good guy in the white hat and quickly carried it as far as he could by wearing an entire white outfit—a costume perhaps not completely conducive to rounding up cattle in open pasture. Not that his boots ever touched open pasture, of course: whether he was fighting desperados or winning the innocent heart of the local school marm, he wore pristine handmade boots of supple leather or exotic skins, with swirls of colorful, intricate stitching and inlaid decoration. Occasionally these designs were edged with costly silver studs or gems. While Mix can be credited with popularizing this image of the rhinestone cowboy, he was followed quicker than a Dodge City posse by a dozen other fancy-and-fast-shootin', white-hatted good guys who could draw their five-string Gibsons and Martins as neatly as their pearl-handled Colts.

Roy Rogers and Gene Autry—to mention only the best known of the singing cowboys—were perhaps responsible for the most picturesque outfits American heroes had ever worn: crimson shirts with lavender yokes and cuffs; striped drainpipe trousers with edged top pockets and badge-shaped belt loops; hand-tooled leather belts sporting engraved silver buckles; fancy silk bandanas; wide-brimmed hats with turquoise bands; and of course boots of the most intricate designs ever imagined. Their boots featured colorful inlays of state flowers or birds, Aztec designs, star bursts or sun rays and crescent moons, longhorn heads, spread eagles, flames, snakes, playing cards, cactus plants, butterflies, monograms, and virtually anything else a cowboy might observe or consider in his time on the range. Medallions were etched just above the toes, the tops could be scalloped, and there were pull tabs. By comparison, contemporary film heroes look like so many unmade beds.

Boots in dove gray and butter yellow, powder blue and burnt orange, peacock and emerald, black and cherry red, walnut brown and cream, grass green and silver—all of the most ingenious design and unparalleled craftsmanship—were not uncommon during this halcyon period of the singing cowboy. Merely to stitch a monogram was child's play compared to the regal ornateness of the sleek black ostrich hide decorated with climbing scarlet roses or the famous red, white, and blue spread-eagle boots worn by Roy Rogers. In the late 1940s the Lucchese Boot Company of San Antonio made for display forty-eight pairs of cowboy boots, each pair depicting the particular state house, flower, bird, and name of every state in the union. This series of boots is still considered the epitome of the art among the legendary Texas boot makers.

By the early 1960s college campuses across the United States were experiencing an outbreak of what may conveniently be called "Frye fever." The John A. Frye Shoe Company had been founded in 1863—exactly a century earlier—in Marlborough, Massachusetts, and much of its fame rests now, as in the '60s, on the boots it made for soldiers and fighter pilots during World War II. But the company's most popular boot by far is based on an older design for what is termed a "harness boot": a small snub-nosed toe, clunky heel, double sole, and high straight-cut top with a strap and brass ring over the instep in a distinctive heavy, oiled tan leather that has an orange cast. It is, in short, a basic, unadorned, tough leather work boot, and beginning about fifty years ago it achieved a certain chic, becoming gradually pop-ularized by those who couldn't go the whole way with cowboy boots. Tens of thousands of these boots were worn by young men and women during the '70s and '80s as an urban answer to prole footwear.

There are two other boots worth mentioning here: the clas-sic desert boot and the Maine duck boot. The first is a variation of the simple, low-cut, rough leather boot found in many differ-ent cultures. It is made from a sole and two pieces of leather: a front piece that includes the instep, vamp, and tongue, and a wraparound, ankle-high piece that serves as the boot's sides and back. The style is sometimes called a chukka boot, because it was thought to be first used by polo players in India. (In polo, "chukka" is the word for a period of play.)

The desert boot as we know it today was first made by the Irish shoe-making firm of Clarks. Nathan Clark, a son of the founder of the firm, was a soldier during World War II and first noticed these boots being worn by British Eighth Army officers during their down time. These unpretentious, rudimentary boots had been bought in the bazaars of Cairo, after the North Africa campaign in which British field marshal Bernard Montgomery had finally defeated the Panzer Army Africa at the Second Battle of El Alamein. Nathan Clark got himself a pair, and after he was demobilized and returned home, he persuaded his father to produce the boot in small batches with a basic two-part, four-eyelet construction, using the sand suede leather and crepe sole that the younger Clark had seen overseas.

Clarks launched the model at the Chicago Shoe Fair in 1949, and it was an immediate hit. In the next half dozen years the boot became wildly popular, worn by young hipsters and college students alike. It was often accompanied by another item from the British war wardrobe associated with Montgomery: the Gloverall duffle coat he was sometimes photographed wearing. Hipsters wore the boots with drainpipe trousers and sometimes dyed them dark brown or black with liquid shoe polish. This has since become unnecessary because Clarks now makes the boots in those colors as well as others, in addition to the classic sand suede. The boots remain comfortable, inexpensive, casual footwear with a global following.

And finally we come to Leon Leonwood Bean, founder of L. L. Bean, and his now-famous duck boots. Bean was something of an American original: entrepreneur, true New England sportsman, and inventor whose mind had a decidedly practical bent. The story is that he loved to hunt the marshy waters around his home in Brunswick, Maine, and wore traditional oiled leather hunting boots. These boots unfortunately couldn't keep water out for very long, and L. L. usually came home at day's end with cold, wet feet. He put his mind to solving this problem and eventually came up with an idea to stitch a leather upper to a rubber shoe. In 1912, after several attempts, he landed on a model that worked well. He called it his "Maine hunting shoe" and built a nice little business on it.

Almost needless to say, this iconic boot—now usually called a "duck boot," with dozens of imitations—is a true fashion statement today, worn on campuses, runways, and city streets around the globe, as well as marshy ponds in New England. According to the company's website, sales of duck boots reached around a half million pairs by their hundredth anniversary in 2012. Today L. L. Bean sells a range of styles in various colors and materials, some with Gore-Tex, Thinsulate, or shearling linings, but all of them still, as they say, "made in Maine one pair at a time."

3

BOW TIES

I THINK WE'D BETTER CLEAR this up right at the onset: you *can* tie a bow tie. If I hear another grown man say he can't, I'll shoot myself.

Let's try to be rational about this. You tie bows all day long: your shoelaces, packages, those colored twist ties on garbage bags. A bow tie is simply a bow that happens to be tied at the throat. I'm not even going to show you a directional diagram here—I'm not catering to this form of childishness. The only difficult thing about tying a bow tie, when you stop to think about it, is that you're looking into a mirror, so the image is reversed. That's absolutely all.

There's really no excuse. Buy a bow tie (I'll get to that in a paragraph or three), and practice tying it. A certain *sprezzatura* (see Chapter 22) is inherent in the technique. A little looseness, a slight raggedness around the edges, an asymmetrical slant— that's what's wanted. Disheveled elegance. Perfect symmetry is not a goal worth pursuing here. We leave that to the anal retentive.

Which brings me to another point: under no circumstances should you buy a pre-tied bow tie. There is a noticeable difference between a bow tie you actually tie yourself and a pretied one: the pretied ones always look too perfect; the *set* is a bit too symmetrical, too balanced and flawless. And I really do hate to say this, but a pretied bow is one of the most obvious signals among aficionados of dress that you're an amateur.

Nor can you afford to ignore the bow tie, as many of us used to. For most of the second half of the last century, the bow tie was thought to be relegated to tweedy professors, editors, and intellectuals with anarchical leanings. But toward the end of the millennium, along came some decidedly cool young men about town sporting paisley silk bows in bright orange and yellow and peacock blue, or natty polka dots or bold stripes. It was refreshing, even if it was—as I suspect—a reaction to the idiotic notion of the moment: wearing a four-in-hand with a dinner jacket. It isn't that I believe a person who wears a four-in-hand with a dinner jacket should necessarily be flogged and shunned. It's just that the little lemmings who engage in that sort of frivolity haven't a clue. They go where they're told—and they're obviously told by some fashion designers renowned for their global tastelessness—while the bow ties go their own way.

Bows for evening dress are symbols of respect for tradition, but for day wear they're signs of dandiacal individualism, with a certain think-for-yourself tone to them. Maybe that's why we're seeing more of them lately—there's greater individuality in dress today. How to be au courant without being bizarre, interested in the new while still respecting the tried and true, that's what amiable dressers understand.

If you want to wear a bow tie, the thing to understand is *shape*. In the nineteenth century men wore all sorts of neck cloths—the cravat, the shoestring, the stock, and the ascot (most of which are covered in Chapter 1)—but the bow tie was very much on the verge of winning out until the 1880s, when longer ties (the now common four-in-hand variety) began to gain prominence. Since then the bow tie has stabilized its shape into two distinct models, both entirely appropriate. It may seem a bit complicated, but it's really not. The butterfly (sometimes called a "thistle") has a blade with a splayed-out shape to resemble a butterfly's wing. This model may have either a straight or a diamond-pointed end. The batwing (sometimes called a "club") has a straight blade with a square end.

The two basic shapes traditionally found in bow ties aren't a matter of international importance, but they do make allowance for one's individuality. And concern in small matters is a signal always worth sending. For some time now the style has been for a smaller batwing (club) bow in brighter colors, tied loosely to achieve that subtle but perceptive hint of nonchalance. The result is miles away from the stodgy, conservative image bows used to conjure up. Today the attractive mix of old-fashioned bohemianism, intellect, and a bit of boyish playfulness wins the day. "Piquant" is perhaps the word I'm looking for.

As for fabrics, neckwear can and has been made out of every fabric imaginable over the years, but silk certainly is the standard. For more seasonal approaches there's always wool challis for cooler climes and cotton madras for warm weather. More importantly, unlike ready-made four-in-hand ties, bow ties should be *sized*, meaning the strip between the two ends should be adjustable to your proper neck size. Look at the inside of the band, where a strip of measured tape will be sewn with slits in which to insert a metal T-shaped fastener. Ingenious really. Even inexpensive bow ties should have an adjustable buckle.

With all of that said, the most important rule for tying bow ties comes from the lovely little book on neckwear attributed to Balzac, *The Art of Tying the Cravat*: "Whatever style may have been adopted in putting on the cravat, when the knot is once formed (whether good or bad) it should not be changed under any pretense whatever." In other words, fix it and forget it.

4

Business Attire

We all know what they say: don't judge a book by its cover or wine by its label. And we keep saying it because judging by appearances is precisely what we do most of the time. With good reason. We all seem to have less time, fuller agendas, more meetings, longer lists of messages to answer, and networking to be done, flights to catch, and the rest of it. Time is one of the more precious commodities of our work week. Who has the time or stamina to dig deeper into the people we meet for a quick business lunch? It seems to be all grin, spin, thank-you, win-win. We leave the rest to psychiatrists and those more spiritually adept than ourselves.

Funnily enough, until the Industrial Revolution or thereabouts, people had a clear, cut-and-dried way of dealing with such imponderables: they divided their lives into public and private spheres. In public, they dressed and acted for their roles in the social order, and in private they wore and acted as they wanted to with intimates. In the oft quoted advice usually attributed to Lord Chesterfield, "Do not inquire too deeply into the truth of other peoples' appearances. Life is more sociable if one takes people as they are and not as they really are." A bit cynical, you may think, but consider the implications. We know that, during his four-term presidency, there was a general, well-mannered agreement among media reporters not to refer to Franklin Roosevelt's health—an arrangement that, as it turned out, was a very good thing. Could such a well-mannered agreement work today? Probably not.

Richard Sennett, in his very thoughtful study *The Fall of Public Man*, argues that we've lost this helpful distinction between our public and private selves. The blurring of the line has certainly occurred in the all-influential media, where discovery-and-confession seems to be the mode of the day. But this loss of both a reasoned artificial public stance and an intimate, authentic private life plays out across the board, not the least in dress and deportment.

With the Industrial Revolution and the rise of the middle class in large cities that increasingly promoted the renunciation of blatant gorgeousness in dress, people began looking at each other in a different way. As Sennett explains, "People took each other's appearances in the street immensely seriously; they believed they could fathom the character of those they saw, but what they saw were people dressed in clothes increasingly more homogeneous and monochromatic. Finding out about a person from how he looked became, therefore, a matter of looking for clues in the details of the costume."

Dress has always been an integral part of public life; indeed, dress as we know it would not exist today if it weren't for the public sphere. To be sure, there have been many theories over the years about why people wear clothes at all. Some have argued for modesty; some for differentiation between the sexes (which is akin to modesty); others for comfort and protection from the elements, the creation of erogenous zones, that sort of thing. But people actually wear clothes for *status*, a person's place in the social structure. If dressing were for modesty or protection, we could all just zip up in the same ballistic nylon bags. But then some of us would want different colored nylon, wouldn't we? Some would want to show an individual preference, which amounts to a difference. That is, we want to seem special to those around us. We want to show our individual *style*. It seems like a civilized tendency that we want to be recognized as being unique. But in truth, the impulse reveals one of our species's baser instincts. There's a long history of both people dressing above their station in life and other people trying to stop them. The latter comes under the category of sumptuary laws, while the former are called "parvenus," who tend to be looked down on, for understandable—if not exactly good—reasons.

We all fit into the social structure one way or another. In the modern world, an ordered society is what we want, a secure structure that, as I think Jeremy Bentham pointed out, provides the most good for the most people. We believe the first purpose of government is to provide domestic tranquility—nature doesn't seem to provide it in abundance—and we try to construct a society that will provide order to everyone's benefit. Yet some people benefit from this system more than others, and those who feel left behind often try to use the rules of the game to get ahead.

There are two particular aspects of this yearning that have a relevance to clothes. First, clothes have always provided the most obvious approach to definition. There was no question about Louis XIV's status when he walked into the room, dripping in yards of ermine, scarlet velvet plush, and gold embroidery. In a democracy, or even in today's monarchies, we are not so obvious and blatant as all that; our statements are more subtle and egalitarian. But we still want our leaders to look like leaders, and even leaders of the most communistic of societies seem a bit better pressed and dirt-free than the office help.

Yet strangely enough, today the office help is what many professionals look like, no matter their actual position in the pecking order. In the past hundred years or so the most evident movement in dress has been toward comfort, a trend that can be seen in the growing importance of the casual wardrobe and the devolution of tailored garments. For the past half century we've been toying with the idea of getting rid of the suit and tie, a democratic revolution in search of a way to preserve the sense of dignity within the casual wardrobe. The question is, how can we be distinguishingly individual when we're all wearing the same sweatshirt, jeans, and running shoes?

The problem remains: *How* should we be taken? And how should we dress to be taken the way we want? In a corporate setting, perhaps more than another place, dressing is a career tool, a critically important statement of who we are and where we want to be in both our work and our social life. The emphasis on attire and grooming may be subtle or blatant, but the imperative is there—and it's overlooked at one's own peril.

Our appearance is a language and, like other languages, should (1) be suitable to the audience, occasion, and purpose and (2) not send confusing messages. I was reminded of this principle a while back, when an acquaintance of mine had just returned from a trade exhibition in Germany and was telling me how his team—which represented a large industrial concern in the United States—had fared with the competition. "I hadn't realized," he blurted rather bitterly, "how shoddily dressed our guys were. Many of the other international firms, the British, the Scandinavians, the Japanese, were all matched up in well-tailored blazers and company ties, while our guys were wearing any old polyester sports coats and baggy khakis. It was a psychological disaster from the start, and we never regained our composure."

Naturally I told him I wasn't surprised that his team lost the business. (I almost never hate saying, "I could have told you so.") When clothes talk about us, as vaguely or subtly as other forms of communication, they identify us as a member of this or that group, and the language they speak is the language of the group, whether in the broadest sense (such as sociological distinctions) or more specifically (as in jobs that call for distinct uniforms). The important question is: Of which group or groups do we wish to be seen as a member?

Within groups, whether it be a college basketball team or a corporate managerial one, there are always rules, the point of which is to let everyone know who's a member and who's not. Of course there are exceptions and interpretations of the rules, and dressing the part within the group can lead to subtle variations. Subtlety is a major facet of modern dress, as well; just think of the difference in attire between a Renaissance prince and a current president. Leaders of industrialized countries today command enough power to make a Louis XIV pea-green with envy, and yet they dress as though they were simply rather well-off businessmen. Which I suppose you could say in a sense they are.

The result of dressing appropriately to one's goals is, as my friend correctly noted, a psychological one: confidence. Appropriate dress frees us from the anxieties and liabilities of sending negative and confusing messages. And finally, if a man is dressed effectively, confidently, and comfortably, he'll be judged on other criteria—talent, productivity, merit, skill, loyalty—which is the way it should be. This isn't a matter of having an extensive, expensive wardrobe, or being a dandy, or anything else like that. It's a matter of being effective and doing a good job.

I'm not in the habit of giving a lot of fashion advice, because I'm not overly interested in the violently trendy and flamboyant uptick of the moment. (You know there is no rest for the fashionable.) But what I would like to advance here is not technical knowledge—the same old gobbledygook about trouser length and whether your belt buckle should match your cuff links—but rather some practical, hard-won advice about how to dress in a business setting. Technical knowledge is what you put in a cookbook recipe. Practical knowledge is the rest of what the chef knows. Like that know-how, the reflections that follow are not only true—everything I want to tell you is true—but also actual.

OBSERVATIONS

1. Simplicity is generally a virtue. Your clothes should not in themselves be more memorable than you are. They should complement you, not compete with you. Avoid trends, fads, flash,

and gimmicks, all of which draw attention to themselves and away from you.

2. Always buy the best you can afford. It's not only the initial outlay that should be considered, but the longevity and satisfaction that counts. Good shoes last longer than cheap ones and look better when they're old than cheap ones do when they're new. In order to save money, invest in quality.

3. Insist on comfort. If you're uncomfortable in your clothes, you'll make others feel uncomfortable, and no one will do his best. In this day and age, it's not necessary to sacrifice comfort to fashion or dignity.

4. Always dress appropriately to the occasion and company.

5. *Fit* is the most important criterion of dress: consider your body carefully, and aim to accentuate its virtues and minimize its liabilities. A suit made of the best fabric in the world is still a bad choice if it doesn't fit well.

6. As a general rule, never wear anything cheap, fancy, shiny, or synthetic.

7. We still believe that an investment banker should look like an investment banker, and feel slightly squeamish about entrusting our hard-earned money to someone who looks like drug-addled surfer. Not that I've got anything against drug-addled surfers, mind you—I just don't want to invest any of my money with them.

BIG MISTAKES

1. *Being too studied:* everything all matched up makes the uniform obvious, overly fastidious, and blatantly narcissistic. Individuality should be in evidence, quietly.

2. *Wearing too many accessories:* like putting all the china on the table at the same time, it's too busy and signals insecurity. Diana Vreeland wisely said that the key to style is *refusal*. This is particularly true today, when there is such a plethora of wares before our eyes.

3. *Using too many patterns:* like an overloaded electrical circuit, the outfit quickly burns out and calls attention to itself. This is not unlike camouflage, in which lines of objects are blurred in order to mislead our eyes away from distinctions we should be making.

4. *Being too understated:* blandness without indicates blandness within. Unless you're incredibly handsome—as was Cary Grant, who made the low-keyed monochromatic approach to dress his signature—make a subtle, distinguishing gesture in your attire.

GENERAL QUESTIONS

1. Have I developed a clear sense of my own personal style?
This question is pretty basic and gets to such reflections as: Where do my ideas about how I should look come from? How do I think others see me? Do I consider my assets and liabilities when shopping for clothes? What sort of an image—and, thus, set of values—do I want to project? Are the components of the image I wish to convey in harmony with each other? And is my image in balance with my professional and social life as well as my personality?

2. For the corporate businessman: Does my personal image reflect my company's image and product or service? Do I understand the global implications of the company and its image?
While individuality is something to be prized and nurtured, we should all be scrupulous to signal our affiliations. If you accept a job with a large law firm and the other lawyers wear suits, the sartorial ground has been laid for you, and those who rock the boat must be aware that other passengers will try to throw them overboard. Upholding the standards of the team is paramount.

3. How do I buy my clothes?

Purchases have a way of becoming ingrained habits early on, psychological traps from which it can difficult to extricate oneself. Questions that lead to self-awareness: Do I buy my own clothes, for how long have I done this, and do I feel comfortable with the process? Why do I shop where I do? Do I consciously coordinate my wardrobe, and how would I characterize it? Am I satisfied and happy with what I wear? When I shop for clothes, do I feel I know what I'm looking for and at? Do I think I know what constitutes quality, how garments should fit, and how to communicate with the sales staff?

4. What are my practical considerations about dressing?

What I mean by "practical" here concerns the actual wearing of clothes. Do I have any fabric allergies? Are there any styles I don't feel comfortable with, I feel I don't look good in, or I don't understand? Are there colors I think are not attractive on me or patterns I think are wrong for me?

PRACTICAL CONSIDERATIONS

1. Mixing Genres of Time

Combine the sleek and modern with great vintage pieces. Show that you take a certain pride in Old World craftsmanship, in objects that have stood the test of time, in style rather than momentary fashion trends. Don't imitate the past; just show that you value it.

2. Mixing Genres of Place

Great dressers like to play genres off against each other, like wearing an old Barbour hunting parka with a city suit or a well-tailored tweed jacket with jeans. There's nothing wrong at all with a bright checked shirt under a somber suit, a vivid grenadine tie with a trad blazer. Gianni Agnelli, a great dresser if there ever was one, liked to wear hunting boots with a town suit. Which brings up a related point: these days, the "uniform"—the old business outfit of dark suit, white shirt, nondescript tie, and black wingtips—is worn by choice rather than obligation.

3. Mixing Labels

Simply put: guys who dress head to toe in a particular designer's gear are thought to be without any taste or imagination of their own.

4. Globalization

Today we seem to be in airports more than at home: it's Hong Kong today and New York, Rio, or Milan tomorrow. We've got to be appropriately dressed in a style that reflects a global level of taste and understanding. International businessmen are dressed for a meeting anywhere. Only those with the absolute confidence that their hometown will remain the world for them can afford to ignore the pressures and influence of globalization.

5. Attitude

Is there any reason why a man shouldn't enjoy his clothes, get pleasure and satisfaction from knowing he's at home in the world and with himself? Be confident about dressing comfortably—but also remember to be appropriate about it. Even pleasure should have its limits.

5

CRAFTSMANSHIP

PEOPLE WHO UNDERSTAND QUALITY buy the best not to spend a fortune but to save one. I first learned this lesson from a great shirt maker, Fred Calcagno. Fred was the owner of Pec & Company and had his small atelier on West Fifty-Seventh Street in Manhattan. He made beautiful shirts and had among his clients Cary Grant, Aristotle Onassis, and several Rockefellers.

I suppose Fred did very well with his business. But what was so fascinating about him was that, like all true craftsmen, he loved what he did and took great pride in his work. He wallowed in small details and concerns, making sure, for example, that the width of a cuff was in proportion to the size of the man's wrist—that sort of thing. One day when I visited him, he was putting new collars and cuffs on a batch of old shirts for a client. The client, as it happened, was one of the Rockefeller brothers. I think it was the one who was, at the time, chairman of Chase Manhattan Corporation.

"It's interesting," Fred mused, "I made these shirts for him ages ago, and every few years he sends them to me to replace the frayed collars and cuffs with new ones. It's a good idea because

33

the bodies of the shirts are like new. He really gets his money out of his clothes." Fred said this, not in any sense of disappointment in not selling his customer a whole new batch of shirts, but as a compliment to a man who understood quality. And that's the difference between a craftsman and a salesman who just wants to sell you something. A real craftsman's interested in making both his product—and you—*better*.

Books on the idea of craftsmanship seem to fall into two categories. Some are academic philosophical-sociological texts of a higher complexity, while others cover terribly specific subjects, such as how to make horseshoes for fun and profit. My goal here is to say a few, much simpler words about craftsmanship, not from either of these positions, but rather in the spirit of the endeavor itself. I've known my share of artisans in the clothing field—tailors, shoemakers, shirt makers, and the like—and have found that the craftsmen's atelier is indeed a fascinating place.

There are, I should hasten to point out, several books on the subject I think are very readable and very much worth reading. My particular favorite book about craft is Thomas Girtin's marvelously written *Makers of Distinction: Suppliers to the Town & Country Gentleman* (Harvill Press, 1959). It's a wonderful journey into the past of those artisans who supplied the English gentleman with his wardrobe and sporting equipment. When, for example, he talks about the great shoemakers and tailors of London and their shops, you can smell the leather and the heathery tweed. This is a rare glimpse of an all-but-bygone world.

Certainly more academic, but readable nevertheless, is Richard Sennett's *The Craftsman* (Yale University Press, 2008). Sennett, a renowned sociologist, argues that the craftsman is an artist who connects his highly skilled physical labor to an ethics of work that we've all but lost. It's a fascinating study that discusses at length what it is that craftsmen actually do and why we should honor their values today.

And finally, I've very much enjoyed a memoir by Aldo Lorenzi, *That Shop in Via Montenapoleone* (Ulrico Hoepli Editore, 2008). Lorenzi's father founded a cutlery shop in Milan in 1929, and it remained *the* most famous place in the world to buy razors and knives and other implements of all sorts until it closed in 2014. This book is a testament of a knife grinder's son from the Rendena Valley—where historically every family had a knife grinder—who has strong beliefs about the place of craftsmanship in the world.

While I'm at it, I'd also like to recommend the beautiful film *O'Mast*, directed and produced by Italian documentary film maker Gianluca Migliarotti. This is a simply wonderful study of the art of tailoring from the Neapolitan perspective. Migliarotti makes the excellent choice of letting these expert craftsmen speak for themselves, and they are incredibly articulate about their profession and art. This is truly an inspiring work of film.

My own thoughts about craftsmanship take me back to a letter written by the nineteenth-century German poet Heinrich Heine about a holiday walking tour of the cathedrals of France he made with a friend. Along the way, he wrote letters home describing the tour, and at their last stop at the majestic, massive cathedral of Amiens, he recorded the conversation: "When I lately stood with a friend before Amiens Cathedral, he asked me how it happened that we can no longer build such works. I replied: Dear Alphonse, men in those days had *convictions*. We moderns have *opinions*. It requires something more than opinions to build a cathedral."

I don't think it's too much of a stretch to say that those men and women who labor, train, and practice a craft, who work at a particular skill until their hands, hearts, and brains are as one, continue that tradition of a loving vocation not unlike the cathedral builders. It's the same approach, and we might say that the emotional investment is not dissimilar either, because there is a real difference between a passion for quality, for making something as perfectly as it can be envisioned and executed, and simply making as much of it as you can as quickly as you can. This is a true and actual difference.

Let me be specific about this. I once visited a famous shirt maker in Milan. The shop was a model of Old World charm: old Persian carpets and mellow wainscoting; bolts of fine cottons, linens, and silks stacked on shelves that went to the ceiling; vintage brass wall sconces. The owner and I chatted away about the finer points and intricacies of constructing the perfect shirt, while over in the corner I noticed an aged man—in his late eighties, perhaps early nineties—stooped over a large wooden board resembling a drafting table, cutting out patterns of cloth with a large shears. It turned out this was the owner's father, and would I care to meet him? I certainly would, I said, and was promptly introduced.

The older gentleman's eye and hand were steady, the workmanship immaculate and beautifully executed. I speak no Italian, and I asked the son to translate a question to his father for me: What is the secret to making such beautiful shirts? They exchanged a few sentences, and the son chuckled and then said to me, "My father says to tell you that he cuts the cloth with love."

For the jaded and cynical, this answer will probably not suffice. But it does for me, because it actually says a great deal about how the craftsman thinks and how he regards his work, his customer, and himself. There is indeed a pride in making something as perfectly as you can and an indescribable satisfaction in having done so. And of course for the clothing craftsman, there is the great satisfaction in the relationship you have with your customers, in making them look and feel better about themselves. These relationships have outlasted marriages and gone along more comfortably as well.

A famous observation about the differences between artisanal work and modern mass production is worth quoting here: "There is hardly anything in the world that someone cannot make a little worse and sell a little cheaper, and the people who consider price only are that person's lawful prey." The operative word here is "lawful." The law, in its great democratic wisdom, assumes that we are all capable of education and that we are

also responsible for our own daily welfare, and let the buyer beware. In their commitment to and passion for quality—for trying to make the best—and for wedding form to function in the most satisfying way we can imagine, and for refusing to be content with the shortsighted and shoddy, these artisans deserve our respect, admiration, and allegiance.

6

DENIM

THERE'S SO MUCH ALREADY WRITTEN about denim that it's hard to know where to begin. But where I want to begin is Milltown, New Jersey. Odd, you might think—let me hasten to explain.

There have been many theories to explain the popularity of the cloth called "denim" (from de Nîmes, the French town and exporter of the cloth in the nineteenth century), and the trouser garment variously called denims, dungarees (from the Hindi *dungri*), jeans (from *Genes*, Old French for Genoa), and Levi's (after Levi Strauss, an itinerant merchant and American clothing manufacturer, not to be confused with Lévi-Strauss, the French social anthropologist and leading exponent of the theory of structuralism, but you know that). Some credit denim to the California Gold Rush of 1849, an event that prompted Strauss, the young Bavarian clothing and cloth peddler living in New York, to move to San Francisco in the hope of selling his wares to the quickly growing population of miners. Others point to Theodore Roosevelt and the rise of the national park system, which opened the West to curious vacationers and exposed them to what people in the West were wearing.

And then there are the proponents of the theory that the popularity of jeans began in the United States in the period between the world wars, when the West began to be heavily populated, dude ranches sprang up as vacation retreats, country music came into its own, and the image of the cowboy became romanticized as the days of the long cattle drive closed forever behind the Industrial Revolution. What became the workwear of one generation became the playwear of the next, just as the work of one generation can become the play of the next.

Actually, this is where my theory, and New Jersey, come in. It's really just an idea, you understand, but I'm calling it a theory to make it sound a bit more impressive. I don't mind talking about the Industrial Revolution, the opening of the West, Yellowstone vacations, and Montana dude ranches, but my instinct is that the romantic image of the cowboy began with an ingenious man named Edwin S. Porter. Porter directed and photographed the first Western action film—a twelve-minute reel called *The Great Train Robbery*—in May 1903. It's a delightful irony that this seminally important Western was actually filmed in Milltown, New Jersey, among the scrub trees of the Pine Barrens about a half hour east of the state capitol of Trenton.

From what I can tell, the popularity of the Western film genre created the interest in western clothes. Jeans, cowboy boots, ten-gallon Stetsons, buckskin ranch jackets, fancy bandanas, and all the rest of it are there in the Westerns from the beginning. And the history is long. *The Great Train Robbery*, which made Broncho Billy Anderson an early cinema star, was soon followed by *The Squaw Man*, a directorial job that made a household name of Cecil B. DeMille and was a huge success in 1913. By the time Gary Cooper—who, along with John Wayne, was Hollywood's quintessential cowboy star—made *The Virginian* in 1929 (he'd already appeared in more than half a dozen other Westerns before the "talkies" were invented), actor-cowboys such as Tom Mix and William S. Hart had been making a great deal of money working in the genre for a decade, and the golden age of the

Western was well under way. From John Ford's mournful use of Utah's Monument Valley to Sergio Leone's dusty spaghetti sagas, the Western has constituted a major film genre and produced some of our greatest movies: *The Plainsman, Stagecoach, Shane, High Noon, The Searchers, Red River, One-Eyed Jacks, High Plains Drifter,* and *Unforgiven,* to name merely a handful of the best. Cowboys in these films were either what was called the "drugstore" variety—Roy Rogers and Gene Autry, in fancy embroidered shirts, ornately designed boots, and white hats—or the more realistic variety, who wore the unadorned jeans and rough boots that equipped real cowboys for life on the plains.

Denim, the indigo-dyed, sturdy twill cloth of France and India, first popularly appeared on the forty-niners digging for gold around Sutter's Mill in Northern California. Levi Strauss—this story is well-known and documented—had taken bolts of heavy canvas west with him, thinking all those transplanted miners would need tents. As it happened, tents didn't sell, but pants did, and entrepreneurial Levi turned his canvas to good purpose. He had his canvas made up into trousers, and when the canvas ran out, Levi wired back to his brothers in New York, and they sent bolts of indigo-dyed French cotton (from Nîmes).

The only important change between the trousers Levi was selling in the 1860s and those worn today was provided, so legend has it, by a Nevada tailor named Jacob Davis. Davis wrote to Levi (I only use his first name because apparently that's how he was known; otherwise we'd call the trousers Straussers, no?) in 1872 and told him he could improve the tough trousers by putting copper rivets at the pocket corners and other stress points. He and Levi took out a joint US patent on the design the following year. Oh, and Levi also started using the orange-stitched double arch on the back pockets that year too. It's said to be the oldest used trademarked logo of any American garment.

Apart from these few modifications, the Levi's you buy today are pretty much what you'd have bought over a century ago: roughly eleven-ounce, indigo-dyed cotton twill with two front

J-shaped pockets, the right one with a small change pocket, and two rear patch pockets with the chevron design; with copper rivets at the stress points, a metal-shank button fly, and all sewn with heavy orange-colored thread. The cut is trim and straight with a short front rise and slightly longer back rise, and a selvage line down the outseam. Levi's are susceptible to change but not improvement: forget the variations that have come and gone over the years; these are the Real Thing.

The modern history is easily followed. Before designers got into the jeans market back in the 1970s, there were basically only three independent denim pants producers in the United States: Levi Strauss, Wranglers, and Lee. Every young man instantly knew the difference by looking at the design on the back pockets—Levis had the double arch, Wranglers a *W*, and Lee a double wavy line—and each brand had its aficionados. And here the story divides.

In the late 1940s and early '50s, there were two sorts of young men who wore jeans: those who favored the western look, and those who took up the rebel look. This was not a clever bit of PR or engineered marketing strategy, but a real difference of style, for the wearers belonged to different worlds. The accessories that accompanied the jeans told the story. The western look included flannel cowboy shirts with yoked back and pearl snaps, inlaid cowboy boots, and belts with fancy western buckles. The rebel look was comprised of leather motorcycle jackets (usually black), engineer boots (always black) with curved heels and cleats, tight T-shirts, and "garrison" belts (two-inch-thick, cowhide military-style belts with heavy metal buckles). The western heroes wanted to ride a horse, the rebel antiheroes a Hog (the nickname for the big Harley-Davidson). Jeans had gone from being country wear to being an urban uniform for postindustrial youth.

But these two types also had much in common. Jeans were always worn low-slung at the hips and rolled up in a thick, three-inch cuff that showed the selvage down the leg seams. This was true of both prototypical icons: John Wayne in *Hondo* and Marlon Brando in *The Wild One* (interestingly enough, these two

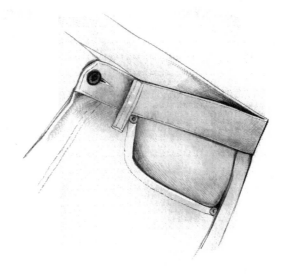

films were made the same year, 1953). Both men had a walk that could only be called a swagger and an attitude somewhere on the cusp of brash, a provocative stare and the laid-back, brooding, cool demeanor of *nil admirari* that was the aesthetic of both the American western hero and the rebel as existential prole hero. Jeans had that sensual, wanderlust effect on young men. It was a look that youth around the world would soon appreciate and appropriate.

The tradition of the young antihero was born with Brando and James Dean, Beat writer Jack Kerouac, and rebel rock stars like Elvis Presley, Gene Vincent, and Eddie Cochran. In *The Wild One*, Brando's denim jeans and black leather jacket identify him as a challenger of society as much as his sneer of insolence. When asked, "What are you rebelling against?," his character Johnny languidly answers, "What've ya got?" For the disaffected, and those posing as such, it was the coolest, hippest utterance ever made: if you were truly hip, you understood there was a systemic corruption of the whole culture. Take a look at Allen Ginsberg's scorching poem *Howl* to get the full flavor of the sense of disenfranchisement. It was as strong as copper rivets and unwashed denim.

Sociologists (and I) like to point out that in contemporary life fashion starts in the street rather than at the top of the social ladder, as it had done for all of its prior history. And denim has been a mainstay of dress for the underclass—Marx's proletariat—ever since its invention. That's what "blue collar" means: cheap cotton dyed blue, as opposed to fine white cotton and linen. After World War II, prole gear became the uniform of that new class in society: the teenager, particularly what came to be known as the "juvenile delinquent." That mix of army surplus, western wear, and cheap laborer's outdoor clothes—denim ranch jackets and engineer boots, T-shirts, wool plaid lumbermen's coats, the iconic Schott black leather motorcycle jacket, G.I. khakis, peacoats, the Willis & Geiger brown cowhide bomber jacket, nylon windbreakers, thick brown leather garrison belts, field parkas, sailor's watch caps, and chambray work shirts—were all bargain priced at army and navy stores that sprung up after 1945 to handle the war surplus. The stuff was well-made and cheap, and the look was too cool to care.

In both Westerns and rebel films of the 1950s there were plenty of jeans. What was essentially different was the film's view of the protagonist. Jeans were associated with and became symbolic of the antihero. In *Shane* (1953), it isn't the soft-spoken traditional hero Alan Ladd who wears jeans when he comes to save the community: he wears buckskins, which differentiate him from others and signal that he is in fact a mythic stranger, albeit within the sartorial traditions of the classic Western. Jack Palance, the hired gun and cold-blooded killer, wears denim. In *The Wild One*, protagonist Marlon Brando rides into a small town, too, but in this case to destroy it or, if not to destroy it, at least to make clear that he has dropped out of the traditional American value system now considered to be a prison of corporate consumerism. The last rebel in this particular genealogy of antiheroes is Steve McQueen. After McQueen's fairly realistic portrait of a rodeo cowboy in *Junior Bonner* (1972), we move into nostalgia, sentimentality, and parody with stars such as John Travolta in *Grease* (1978), the classic caricature of the rocker rebel, released less than twenty-five years after a young man named Elvis walked into Sam Phillip's Sun Studio to make a recording for his mother.

It's really a short step from the angry young men of the '50s to the counterculture youth movement of the '60s and '70s. The "drop out" message was already there; all you had to add was drugs, metallic rock, and perhaps a smattering of New Left political philosophy, and you get the flower-powered hippie generation. Jeans changed along with the times, reflecting both the revolutionary and the divided aspects of the '60s and '70s. It was students on the elite campuses at Berkeley and Columbia, not Monument Valley or *On the Road*, who sparked the fashion; these jeans were bell-bottomed and tie-dyed, purposefully patched and stonewashed, meticulously distressed designer denim by Ralph and Tommy and Calvin. And the outlaw iconography became diluted with ersatz folk songs about suffering. Jeans were reduced to a mere shadow of their former selves, and about these reworked rebellious symbols was the sour smell of self-conscious irony. Brando and Dean, at least we thought at the time, would never have sacrificed authenticity for celebrity. We look in vain for the truth in denim today. Acid-washed or preworn, Japanese selvage or American-made Spandex-cotton blends, our jeans reflect our modern world in all its complexity and, more often than not, vacuity. The product of rigorous effort rather than natural taste. But true elegance is made of sterner stuff, and the real jeans are someplace out there in the Pine Barrens—out where New Jersey meets the Wild, Wild West.

7

DRESSING GOWNS

IN 1622 ANTHONY VAN DYCK, the renowned painter to
the English court of Charles I, was commissioned to produce
a portrait. His subject was Sir Robert Shirley, who had traveled
extensively in the Near East and was Persian ambassador at the
Court of St. James's. Shirley posed for van Dyck wearing a large
silk turban and an ornate silk, calf-length gown thrown over his
shoulders. It was a pose of calculated deshabille and one of the
earliest indications of the modern dressing gown—or *robe de
chambre*, if you will.

The "chamber robe" has a long and storied history. From the
Middle Ages until well into the sixteenth century in Europe,
men found relief from their stiff, heavy doublets and tunics by
simply wearing either a loose shirt in warm weather or an over-
robe against the cold. But during the seventeenth century, men
took to wearing house gowns, which were more ornate versions
of the simple muslin nightgowns they wore for bed.

Growing trade and exploration of the Near and Far East increased during this period; English interest heightened after
mid-century, when Charles II received the island of Bombay as
part of the dowry of Catherine of Braganza. Exotic dress became

the fashion for at-home wear, as did other exotic imports such as tea and chocolate, porcelain, and chintz. Samuel Pepys, whose exacting diary provides much of our knowledge of the period, bought his first dressing gown on July 1, 1661. "This morning," he recalled, "I went up and down into the City to buy several things (as I have lately done for my house): among other things, a fair chest of drawers for my own chamber and an Indian gown for myself. The first cost me 33s, the other 34s."

We can infer the importance of the gown as an article of clothing from its price alone: it cost Pepys more than the piece of furniture! That these gowns were expensive and much-prized possessions is also evident from the fact that men frequently sat for their portraits wearing elaborately patterned dressing gowns. Pepys himself wore a golden-brown silk Indian gown when he sat for his portrait by John Hales in 1666.

These informal "house" gowns were never considered strictly correct for wear out of doors. Men wore them to relax privately at home, accompanied by a soft skull cap or turban and slippers (so both heavy wigs and boots could be removed for comfort). Originally called Persian, Turkish, or Indian gowns because of their Asian origin and design, later terminology points to their usage: bed gown, morning gown, night gown, dressing gown. They were cut kimono-like and loose, full-length, with flowing sleeves, and were first made of brightly printed cottons, then in silk brocade, damask, and velvet.

An alternative style, called a "banyan" (*banian* was the Portuguese word for a Hindu and came into European languages through the East Indian trading companies), became popular in the second half of the century and was considered very fashionable throughout the eighteenth century. The banyan-style dressing gown made for English banker Thomas Coutts (1735–1822) of dotted heavy flannel, doubtless to keep out the cold, had a more fitted, three-quarter length and slightly flared shape with narrow, cuffed sleeves and standing collar. The looser models were often worn wrapped over and closed with a sash, while the more fitted banyan ones typically had frogged button closures. They were sometimes quilted for warmth.

Up through the eighteenth century, as men's day dress began to simplify into what would eventually become the somber suit of the nineteenth century, the dressing gown remained exotic domestic attire in which men could take their ease with their families or receive guests as a sign of intimacy for levees or for the evening. They were particularly useful garments in the early nineteenth century, when the morning toilette for gentlemen could stretch into several hours. That consummate dandy George "Beau" Brummell regularly spent the whole morning bathing, grooming, and dressing, preparatory to a stroll, sporting event, or visit to his club. Often his levees attracted an appreciative audience that included the Prince of Wales.

The Regency gentleman's dressing gown was a loose wrap reaching to the ground, sashed at the waist, and made of ornately printed cashmere, Indian silk brocade, or heavy damask, often in a paisley design. By mid-century this style had evolved to its modern conformations: the usual model was cut with broad, rolling lapels and deep sleeve cuffs, both usually quilted, and a tasseled sash. The accompanying soft cap often had an identical tassel.

While this style shared its domestic popularity after 1870 with a short, hip-length coat—called a "smoking jacket" because it was typically worn at all-male gatherings convened after dinner for the purpose of convivial cigar and cigarette smoking— the form and details continue with us today, combining utility with beauty. Today they are still the perfect garment for lounging around the house or entertaining good friends.

There are still fine shops specializing in wonderful dressing gowns, and fashion-conscious men are still as thoughtful in choosing their robes as any other part of their wardrobes. Awhile back I cocurated at the Museum of the Fashion Institute of Technology an exhibition on the 1930s, which featured a particularly stunning silk dressing gown made by the French firm of Charvet: heavy, antique, yellow damask silk, embroidered with a chinoiserie motif of the silk road, and featuring black satin lapel facings and a sash with ornate tasseled ends. It was a magnificent modern version of what Pepys wore three centuries previously. Charvet is of course very much still in business today and continues to make magnificent dressing gowns.

8

THE ENGLISH
COUNTRY HOUSE LOOK

EXPERIMENTING WITH "LOOKS" can be very expensive. The Gothic business look (laser-cut sharp black suits and pointed shoes), the neo-preppy Japanese look (a carefully curated mix of Ivy style and prole gear), the Neapolitan relaxed elegance look (crumpled linen), the urban guerrilla look (army-navy surplus), and on and on. Which one is more *you*?

May I suggest taking one step forward by taking two steps backward: the tried and true English country house look (ECHL). It has stood the test of time, has proven adaptable to virtually any body shape, continues to have enviable street creds globally, and can be worked and reworked over and over again to suit a person's age and mood, position in life, and occasion ad infinitum.

Many British writers have pondered the magic of the English room as a decorating subject—Evelyn Waugh, Vita Sackville West, E. F. Benson, and James Lees-Milne have all written about English interior decorating—but in his distinctive book, *On Decorating*, the American decorator Mark Hampton puts his finger on the secret of the English country house look:

Rooms with old worn carpets and turn-of-the-century uphol-
stered furniture which, instead of being newly reupholstered,
is covered in loose slipcovers that look (and perhaps are) home-
made. There are books everywhere and leather club fenders in
front of smoke-streaked mantelpieces. This is commonly called
the undecorated look. Sometimes it is the result of happen-
stance; sometimes a subtle effort has been made to design a
timeworn atmosphere.

"Sometimes a subtle effort" sounds like the perfect title for a
study of the ECHL. The whole idea of this canny approach to
decor is to give the impression that strata of taste have been laid
down over the years by successive owners and that its crowded
incongruities are the result of a collective history. That's what
gives the look its authenticity as a document of taste—as though,
as novelist E. F. Benson put it, "each stratum of taste had been
deposited there as by a natural and geological process." It's not
a question of being "period"—the kind of thing mediocre deco-
rators love—but a disarrangement of things, like Regency chairs
and Georgian carpets and Victorian sideboards all in a mad mix.
Everything is muddled up.

It's often pointed out by historians that the British have no
history of a centralized royal court from which to direct social
behavior—as opposed to, for example, France's long experiment
with centralized government at Versailles, which lasted from
the early 1660s until the revolution in 1789 and set the tone of
French aristocracy for much longer. Ordinary Britons, by contrast, had no single, accepted standard for comportment, dress,
and that sort of thing—a fact that can be seen in the slightly
madcap style of many British country homes today.

The British aristocracy preferred to stay on their country es-
tates and came up to London when it was necessary. Country
houses meant country clothes—hunting and riding clothes made
of sturdy fabrics, not the silks and satins surrounding royalty.
This upper-class penchant for country living was furthermore

conjoined in the seventeenth and eighteenth centuries with a growing middle-class mercantile trend toward a renunciation of frivolous dress. Costume historian David Kuchta explains: "In calling upon gentlemen to reform their luxurious ways, mercantilists merged nationalist ideology with gender ideology, creating an image of masculinity compatible with English commodities and English values. . . . The argument for free trade was nothing if not an attack on aristocratic control: free trades portrayed aristocrats as effeminate fops living in luxury, monopolizing consumption of consumption."

What this meant for modern British style was that, while the pressure of instilling uniform codes for business continued, there was an eccentric country style that continued among the gentry apart from the concerns of the bourgeoisie. The mercantile style of Victorian Britain became the universal business uniform, but it was the eccentric style of the gentry that became known as the quintessential ECHL that survives today.

Eccentric? True enough, and what is superficially perceived isn't thematically neat or even intellectually safe. But what is more deeply perceived is even more important: a respect for

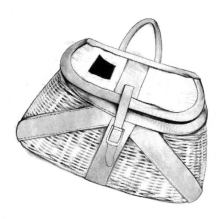

preservation and compromise, an inherent underlying stability that one finds in long-established homes. They're decorated to look as if they've never been decorated. And perhaps not as openly discussed, what applies to the appearance of the interior domestic decor applies to the appearance of the inhabitants as well.

Since any number of designers have already made a tidy living with their ideas about "lifestyle decorating," let's discuss the two true markers of the ECHL—and, by extension, some ways you can attain it.

First, it's critical to remember that shabbiness is preferred to newness. New is vulgar; the mildly tatty is preferable to the new and shiny. Flaunting new labels, or any label for that matter, gives the impression of insecurity. A faded, slightly patinated atmosphere is ideal in achieving a timeless, understated look that bespeaks craftsmanship and the right proportions. The renowned tailoring firms of Savile Row, for instance, still tend to feel that they've failed a customer somehow if he gets complimented for wearing a new suit. Clothes aren't supposed to be worn as though they were objects in themselves; they're the extensions of the individual body and the mind. All of which means that missing buttons or frayed cuffs, a few stains and patches are all to the good. Rumpled but expensive is what we're going for here, the crumble-down approach in which nothing is ever really in or out of fashion. Only old and broken-in tweed sports jackets have leather elbow patches or cuff binding. New clothes may have beauty, but they have no sentiment or real pedigree. New clothes only have labels. (To be sure, there's an aspirational gentility about this, but Ralph Lauren has firmly convinced us over the years that our grandfathers all owned mahogany-lined speedboats and polo ponies, even though they were laboring away in some steel mill. You can't beat the past as a commodity. *Downton Abbey* rather than Downtown.)

Second, prepare by cultivating the impression of never having prepared. Obvious coordination is to be avoided at all costs. Ties,

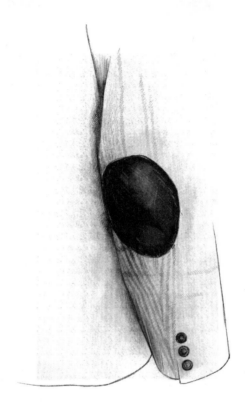

socks, and pocket squares should slightly clash at the very least. Wearing clothes from different genres—or different periods or occasions—is helpful. Town and country often meet in the truly assured. Combining an old pair of striped morning trousers with a blazer and slightly dilapidated cricket sweater works well. A town suit with a well-worn Barbour jacket, or mossy sheepskin and misshapen trilby (slightly too small), or porridge-thick tweeds worn with a very proper town shirt and dotted silk tie—all these achieve the effortless effect. Untidiness trumps symmetry and organization every time, and the unpredictable incongruity that seems so erratically natural is inspirational. Unity of style is no virtue at all; it's the "engaging agglomeration of different styles," as Vita Sackville-West put it, that's really the ticket. This is really the oldest form of the too-cool-to-care pose, the hautest form of reverse snobbery.

But the truth is, civility in all its forms depends on little lies, and sometimes the subtlest effort is necessary to achieve the most natural of appearances. Don't take my word for it. Just ask Ralph.

9

EVENING DRESS

I'VE NEVER BEEN A BELIEVER IN the theory that everything new is old, that things keep coming back, that trends
are cyclical. But not long ago the *New York Times* caused me
to rethink this whole thing. According to fashion reporter Guy
Trebay and the designers he quotes in the article, the tuxedo is
back. Let me restate that to make it clear: after casual Fridays
when otherwise astute professional men turned up at the office
wearing cargo shorts, after celebrities of every stripe began showing up at awards ceremonies without neckwear, after you could
no longer see a pair of polished leather shoes on city streets, and
after the T-shirt seemed to be acceptable even at weddings and
funerals, *the tuxedo is back!*

And not only back, but *really* back. The most pregnant evidence is that J. Crew, the firm that, under the direction of
Frank Muytjens (head of design), has been moving steadily into
tailored clothing and its accessories, is producing a full line of
tuxedos. Who would have thought? (Well, I would, but never
mind—I'll get back to that.) Mr. Muytjens is quoted in the article saying, "Guys are ready to dress up a little more, but on
their own terms. . . . I want to take the tuxedo out of the world of

stuffy formal men's wear. To me it's just a sports coat with peak lapels." Fair enough.

Perhaps it's precisely because men don't *have* to wear a suit or tuxedo that they may *want* to wear an outfit like that. It's now become a very individual kind of expression. A fertile field for a bit of sociology.

All these efforts to revive the tuxedo notwithstanding, the twentieth century will be seen as its greatest age. From the last two decades of the nineteenth century to the end of the following one, the tuxedo has had an incredibly long shelf life and kept its intrinsic form intact. And for very good reasons. Clothing is a bit like architecture in that it tries to solve problems of living, and those attempts that don't work are eventually discarded. The tuxedo has *worked* for a very long time. It has a durable track record.

In its basic form, its simplicity and variations—in terms of color, design, silhouette, and fabric—have been for the most part subtle. The tuxedo consists of matching coat and trousers made of a smooth-finished black fabric. (Here I'm using the American term; the British name is "dinner jacket"; on the European continent, *le smoking*. Both are synecdoches, in which a part stands for the whole, leading to sometimes bizarre grammatical expressions such as "I can't find my dinner jacket trousers.") The coat traditionally aims for stark simplicity with a single-buttoned front—although double-breasted versions having either two, four, or six buttons have been acceptable since the 1930s—with a minimum of decoration and evening dress trousers that are equally austere. The goal is minimalist simplicity. Early evening trousers were even devoid of pockets.

All in all, the tuxedo and its attendant accessories have been considered the most restrained and prescribed attire in a man's wardrobe for over a hundred years. And since the tux is used sparingly, the impression is rather like watching a long series of color films and then seeing something in black and white: startlingly elegant. The outfit has been historically seen as a completely dignified foil to the more colorful dress worn by women. Not perhaps an appropriate interpretation today, but in practice still vigorously maintained. Formal dress is not the place for laissez-faire aesthetics.

You can begin almost anywhere when talking about the history of formal wear. In his readable and informative book, *Men in Black*, John Harvey notes that Chinese emperors as far back as the eleventh century BCE wore black tunics to proclaim their worthiness and that both Greeks and Romans of ancient times donned black togas for serious occasions. During the early Christian era in Europe members of the clergy wore black; think of the Black Friars.

These ancient precedents notwithstanding, the modern history of serious black clothing really begins with Renaissance Spain in the early sixteenth century. From the portraiture of the era and its instructional books of manners, we can note that black clothing was thought to have more grace and sobering propriety about it. Both Charles I of Spain (1500–1558) and his son Philip II (1527–1598) took to black as the uniform of power and authority. And when kings take up something, it becomes prudent for courtiers to follow—so black clothing slowly would have filtered down to royal subjects in this way. As Spanish rule pushed north and east into the Netherlands and Italy, so did black as the mark of official dignity. It surely helped that Charles I became Holy Roman emperor in 1519, retitling himself Charles V and pushing his sartorial preferences on an even greater number of subjects.

The portraits of Spanish royalty by Diego Velazquez in the seventeenth century clearly reveal this tendency, as does the golden age of Dutch portraiture of the following century. By then, Holland was a world power, and hundreds of Dutch merchants, professional men, public bureaucrats, and members of the aristocracy had their portraits painted for immediate gratification and posterity wearing their best black worsteds and silks with white lace collars and cuffs. Black had indeed become the somber symbol of serious men doing serious work. Gerard ter Borch's *Portrait of a Young Man*, painted around 1660, is a handsome indication of the form and character of the style. The young man has an expression of quiet self-importance and dignity, heightened by a simple backdrop of table and chair. He's dressed completely in black, from his silk-ribboned, square-toed shoes to his high-crowned, broad-brimmed hat. His shirt, the sleeves of which are set off by black arm garters, and lace over-collar are sparkling white linen.

Interestingly enough, and with the exception of certain Protestant religious groups such as the Quakers, French and English men of wealth and power continued to be more interested in colorful garb—but that tide would eventually turn as the Industrial Revolution heated up. (See the Introduction for more on this.) The commonly held theory is that black suits came to predominate in a man's wardrobe as the uniform of the middle class, for men who worked in gritty, smoky Victorian cities and manufacturing centers, because they provided a practical way to deal with grime, a needed anonymity, and a regimented uniform for the business section of society. It was, in short, a statement of neutrality for an urban environment.

The Victorian Age saw the triumph of the black broadcloth suit worn by the new rising business sector of professional businessmen. It was the age when propertied men stopped being "esquires" and started being gentlemen, as well as the beginnings of a mass movement toward sartorial standardization and democratization. And at this point we have the conditions for the making of the tuxedo, if not the actual garment itself. For the slight jump from the black business suit to the tuxedo, we must turn to the Edwardians.

The idea of special dress becoming narrowly prescribed by the time of day took on peculiar proportions during the mid to late nineteenth century. By the time the Prince of Wales had become Edward VII, people were motivated by a seemingly outward propriety as a road to dignity, stability, and respect. Both

men and women dressed specifically for the time of day and occasion to an unprecedented degree. In a telling anecdote, when
a friend showed up to accompany the king to an exhibition of
paintings before lunch wearing a tail coat, Edward angrily told
him, "I thought everyone must know that a short jacket is always
worn with a silk hat at a private viewing in the morning." (Undoubtedly the Edwardians, living in a rapidly changing world not
unlike our own, firmly believed that a rigid adherence to rules
would ensure social, political, and even intellectual equilibrium.
Three years after Edward died, those hopes were shattered in the
mud of Flanders and on the banks of the Somme.)

In those gauzy days at the end of the nineteenth century there
were two types of evening wear for gentlemen: The tail coat, with
its accessories, was always worn for public occasions. And then
there was the less formal, short black coat—the "dinner jacket"—
for private evenings at home. Edward himself liked the idea of
the short jacket and around 1875 or so gave it his imprimatur by
having his tailor Henry Poole (whose namesake company is still
in business today) run one up for him, with black silk facings on
the front of the lapel. There were other versions of this jacket too,
more colorful ones made from cut velvet, some with frogging (the
ornate decoration around buttons and button holes, usually made
of looped braid or cord), sashes (cloth belts, often with fringed
ends), and piping (distinctive piece of satin cording usually placed
at the edges of the garment). After a dinner party, when the ladies had left the table, the gentlemen retired to a private room,
removed their tailcoats, and donned their short smoking jackets
to enjoy cigars and whisky, billiards, and perhaps some risqué pic-
tures and jokes. Eventually the tailcoat was dismissed from this
scene altogether, and the short jacket ruled the evening.

There are several theories about how the short dinner jacket
came to the United States, but they all revolve around Tuxedo
Park, New York, that enclave of the wealthy just north of New
York City. According to the various stories, either Pierre Loril-
lard or James Brown Potter—both members in good standing of

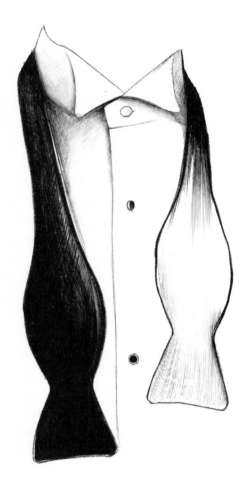

the Tuxedo Park Club—visited England in 1886 and was invited
to a house party at which the Prince of Wales, and perhaps all
the other Englishmen in attendance, wore the short jacket. The
American asked the prince about it, and Edward recommended
him to Henry Poole. On his return to the United States, Loril-
lard or Potter or whoever it was wore the jacket to an event at the
Tuxedo Park Club. Other members soon followed the fashion,
and the "tuxedo" had found a new home in America.

The tux—or dinner jacket, or whatever you want to call it—has
changed very little since that day. The differences and variations

have come about mainly in terms of comfort, a few minor styling details, and some interesting aberrations of color. Until the late 1920s, a gentleman's dress kit consisted of an evening coat and matching trousers of eighteen- to twenty-ounce barathea wool or serge, cotton or linen shirt with heavily starched bosom and stand-up wing collar, silk top hat, and accessories. It added up to around twenty pounds of cloth and starch, tightly cut and stiff as a frozen carp, but the dignity of deportment was insured by the moral superiority that came with enduring the physical burden and constriction of the garment.

Beginning in the 1930s, though, the stuffed sausage look began to change. Central heating, lighter weight fabrics, and a more relaxed social attitude all contributed to making men's clothes more comfortable. And none of this was lost on the then Prince of Wales.

The prince was modern if he was anything: he liked night clubs and jazz, airplanes and golf, travel and sportswear; he also seems to have been particularly fond of married women, but that's not especially modern. Along with several other fashionable members of his set, including his brother the Duke of Kent, Lord Louis Mountbatten, playwright and entertainer Noel Coward, and popular song-and-dance man Jack Buchanan, he was a style revolutionary not unlike Brummell had been a hundred years before. Edward was a modern dandy, eager to throw off the rules of his father's generation, and for evening dress he preferred the short dinner jacket to tails, a double-breasted that obviated the need for either cummerbund or dress waistcoat. He also gave his imprimatur to the soft, turndown-collar shirt. As he explained in his memoir, *Windsor Revisited*, "we began to find that with the double-breasted dinner jacket, a soft collar looked just as neat as a stiff one, and by the thirties we were all beginning to 'dress soft,' thus combining as no previous generation had done, sartorial dignity with comfort and ease." It was a testament to his influence that, when the prince became among the first to wear midnight blue instead of black for dress

evenings, Savile Row tailors were soon deluged with orders for midnight-blue tuxedos.

The 1940s were something of a hiatus for fashion because of the war effort and the use of uniforms. For women, the retro "new look" of Christian Dior—which restored voluminous fabric and color to the female wardrobe—was first seen in 1947, but it took till the 1950s for men to break out into color. The innovations came from all over, but it was Italy that probably had the most sway in European fashion during this period. Italian designers promoted lightweight and colorful, tailored clothes. The "continental look" of the '50s saw tuxedo jackets of mohairs and *doppione* silks in iridescent jewel and parfait colors such as raspberry, French blue, ruby, silver, emerald, claret, and sapphire worn with black dress trousers at resorts and country clubs in warm weather, and tartans in cooler climes. There was also a vogue for patterned cummerbunds and matching bow ties. (Perhaps coincidentally, the era of the black-and-white film was also being rapidly replaced by color during this time.)

It was the beginning of what, in the next decade, would be called the "peacock revolution," and men were now paying attention to a wider range of fashion options. For both daywear and evening wear, primary among them was the neo-Edwardian look promulgated by the British and based on a longer, wasp-waisted jacket that flared out over the hips and narrow trousers in true equestrian style. The style was given wider currency by the French women's wear designer Pierre Cardin, who copied the look for the first-ever designer menswear collection. It's said he himself was a customer of the famed Savile Row tailoring firm of Huntsman, which specialized in that silhouette. Whatever its influence, Cardin's collection was a revolution, and it made him a household name—and a fortune. He's since become the god-father of that first generation of menswear designers that came to include Bill Blass and John Weitz in the United States, Pierre Balmain and Gilbert Feruch in France, Rupert Lycett Green and Tommy Nutter and Hardy Amies in England, and Carlo Palazzi and Bruno Piatelli in Italy.

Meanwhile, the British were busy with their own revolution, called Carnaby Street after the pedestrian mall in London's SoHo neighborhood where it was localized. The look was a more extreme version of the Savile Row equestrian styling, but now in unusual fabrics and colors—bright jewel-toned velvets and brocades—accompanied by fancy printed shirts and matching ties. Trousers as well as the coats flared out at the bottom. Evening wear, which had seemed so pristine and simple since the mid-nineteenth century, suddenly renounced the Great Renunciation and returned to gorgeousness.

The 1970s was a cardiac-arrest period for dress, and—just as in the peacock revolution of the 1960s—evening wear wasn't spared. Tuxedos now were printed velvet, silk-lined denim, lime-green gabardine, and every other atrocity imaginable, accompanied by lace-fringed pastel shirts, floppy ties, and floppier hats. Men vied with women in gorgeousness and ostentation.

It was all too much, and every style invariably contains the seeds of its own destruction. Soon the most radical thing that menswear designers could do was be reasonable. At least that's what the second generation of men's clothing designers seemed to think. Giorgio Armani decided that menswear should be casually elegant and comfortable, while Ralph Lauren saw great value in tradition and classicism. The '80s witnessed a great period of readjustment and international expansion of dress for men. Italian designers and manufacturers gained a firm hold on the upper end of the market, designers proliferated, and the beginnings of a historic change entered both business and evening dress: the casual revolution.

By the '90s businessmen were dressing like their surfer sons to the office and wearing simple tuxedos with casual shoes and either no tie or a four-in-hand for special occasions. Invitations initiated choices and considerable license, such as "creative black tie," "fun formal," "dress optional," or "discretional dress" in accordance with the new spirit of unbridled freedom everyone was feeling—or perhaps afraid of losing. The results were undoubtedly a good deal more physically comfortable for many, but psychologically more disruptive. No one knew exactly *what* to wear on any specific occasion—the options were mind-boggling—and so everyone started to just wear whatever they had on for every occasion. Which meant, in effect, that we had completely lost all sense of occasion. Whatever the event, men from the 1980s onward showed up looking as though they'd just come from the gym.

The turn of the twenty-first century was the age of "too cool to care." The rather obvious example is the TV award shows from this period, at which all the women looked drop-dead glamorous and the men looked as though they couldn't care less and were above it all. The problem was that all we, the viewers, saw was the strain of the effort to be cool.

Thankfully, evening wear seems to have once again landed on its feet. And those feet are wearing natty Albert slippers too! The tuxedo has been recast in a trim silhouette—a closer-fitting body with slightly narrow lapels and slimming trousers—to produce a youthful, lean look. Fabrics are lighter, in the seven- to eleven-ounce range of mohairs, linens, silk blends, and tropical worsteds. Comfort and dignity have been restored.

Some simple rules apply, now and across the ages. The classic tuxedo coat follows the preferred tailored silhouette of the day. If business suits have wider shoulders or narrower trousers, invariably the tuxedo will too. There are, however, subtle differences. Single-breasted dinner jackets usually take only a single button closure, a ventless back, and besom pockets (no flaps), all of which is aimed at providing a more elegant and simpler line. Additionally, the classic dinner jacket never has a notched lapel; either a peak or shawl lapel is considered appropriate, and the choice is strictly a matter of personal preference. The lapels can be faced with smooth satin or ribbed grosgrain (fine-ribbed heavy silk), usually of the same black or midnight blue of the tuxedo fabric itself. Colored or white resort dinner jackets also take the same color facing as their fabric. The idea is to match, not to contrast.

Dress trousers differ from business trousers traditionally in only two respects: they are never cuffed, regardless of the current fashion in day trousers, and a stripe (matching the lapel facings) of either satin or grosgrain runs the length of the outside leg seam. In the past, men wore braces with dress trousers, but this is a matter of fashion and preference. All in all, it's a presentation of elegant sparseness, reminiscent of what Beau Brummell wore two centuries ago.

Evening shirts are traditionally pure white fine cotton or silk and always have pleated bosoms (the rule: the larger the man, the wider the pleats), double or French cuffs (held together with cufflinks), and either a wing or a turndown collar. If a wing collar is chosen, the collar points (the wings) always go *behind* the bow tie. The classic dress shirt has three buttonholes in the middle of the shirt front, for which studs replace the buttons; it's really the only ornamentation called for or needed. Colors, ruffles, lace, patterns, and piping are the purview of the mariachi band.

This brings me to another point, one I've already touched on in Chapter 3: before the so-called casual revolution, an evening tie always meant a bow tie, with either square or pointed ends, in a silk matching the facings of the jacket's lapels. The dandies among us might occasionally opt for polka dots or other patterns and colors, but it takes incredible self-assurance to wear

anything but black or midnight blue. Some men, however, have
of late developed the notion that it's appropriate to wear a satin
four-in-hand tie with a tuxedo, rather than a bow tie. Like most
fashion trends, this was first thought to be terribly hip, then de-
ceptively *now*, and now merely old, sad, haute twaddle; this is
also true for the frighteningly cool "no tie" look, which has the
added distinction of always being done by the wrong people—in
this case, those among us who are hyper-stylish and have a great
deal of misplaced enthusiasm. This bit of nonchalance is just too
obvious to be hip and about as subtle as a beer commercial.

The bow tie might be an evening dress staple, but not all items
are—or at least, not all are so straightforward. For instance, the
cummerbund—that pleated waist sash of Indian origin—has not
survived well. A half century ago virtually every man had one in
his formal wardrobe; today they're merely esoteric relics.

Thankfully, the dress waistcoat is still alive, characterized and
differentiated from the day waistcoat by being low cut, with a
horseshoe-shaped front—with a three-or four-button closure—
to better show off the shirt studs. These waistcoats may also be
backless; many of these style details were invented to reduce
the weight of the outfit. After all, the main entertainment when
wearing a tuxedo was dancing—which also explains why evening
footwear has always been of a light construction.

While I'm on the subject of shoes: those are usually black in
color, fairly unadorned, often low-cut, and worn with plain dark
hose (cotton lisle, fine merino wool, or silk). There is a surpris-
ingly acceptable variety of formal footwear: plain black calf or
patent leather oxfords, velvet Albert slippers, or patent leather
slippers with bows.

Another detail, this one lost somewhat to time: the flower in
the left lapel, the boutonniere, has gone the way of the hansom
cab and the finger bowl. Edwardian tradition quaintly prescribed
only three flowers to adorn the tuxedo: the blue cornflower, the
red carnation, the white gardenia. Today it would be like pre-
scribing a snuff box, spats, or ceremonial sword. But a simple

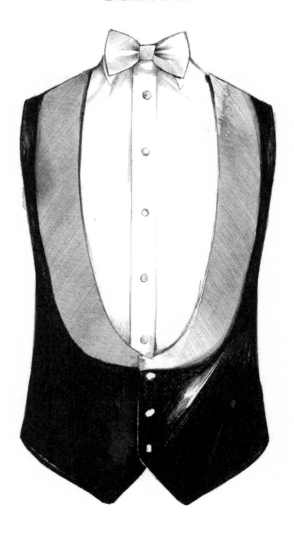

white linen handkerchief in the breast pocket is still considered de rigueur.

Finally, there is one other holdover from a bygone era. This one is still acquiesced to if the invitation states "evening dress— decorations." I'm referring to the wearing of medals, orders, decorations, and miniatures. While full decorations may automatically be worn with white tie and tails, only the ones most appropriate to the particular ceremonial occasion are worn with the tuxedo, and at the discretion of the host. (NB: A boutonniere is never worn with decorations.)

I think that covers just about everything. If not, there are dozens of self-help manuals and etiquette guides out there with up-to-the-minute and down-to-the-button advice. There's plenty of advice around about *what* clothes should be worn, but I've found there is one bit of advice never given in these weighty tomes: *how* the clothes should be worn. To get at this point, let me recall a wonderful story about Noel Coward told by his companion and biographer Cole Lesley.

As a young man of twenty-four, fresh and glowing from his first success as a playwright and actor in *The Vortex*, Noel Coward was invited to join the prestigious Tomorrow Club (which eventually became the famous PEN Club for writers). The membership consisted of the literary lions of the day: John Galsworthy and Somerset Maugham, Rebecca West, H. G. Wells, E. F. Benson, Arnold Bennett, and on and on. But let Lesley pick up the story here: "Not knowing the form, Noel arrived at his first meeting with the Tomorrow Club in evening dress, to find everybody in day clothes. He paused only a moment in the doorway as the eminent heads turned towards him. 'Now I don't want *anybody* to feel embarrassed,' he said."

The real trick to wearing clothes, and this is especially true of evening clothes, is to wear them as if you mean it, while at the same time giving the impression that it's a natural grace. Not like some Prussian general on the reviewing stand, but the way Fred Astaire wore them. Elegant ease and natural assurance—*that's* the way to wear evening dress.

10

EYEWEAR

LET ME STATE WITHOUT UNDUE equivocation: spectacles became popular in 1965. I have no great stake in saying
this; it's simply a fact.

Perhaps I should explain. And let me do so by asking a simple
question: When did film stars start wearing spectacles? I mean
as either male heroes or glamour girls? Since we've all decided,
as a culture, that celebrity is the mark by which to make judgments, this perspective is an eminently fair way to approach the
history of any trend. So let me refresh your memory. It was 1965,
the film was *The Ipcress File*, and the star was Michael Caine,
playing the role of Len Deighton's spy, Harry Palmer. Caine was
so successful in this role, wearing his heavy black Wayfarer-style
plastic spectacles, that he reprised it the next year in *Funeral
in Berlin*. Film critic David Thomson said Caine's performance
"was as cold and barricaded as his spectacles," but the public
seemed to love it, and Caine went on to make *Alfie*, *The Wrong
Box*, *The Italian Job*, *Get Carter*, *The Man Who Would Be King*,
Hannah and Her Sisters, *Mona Lisa*, *Noises Off*, *Little Voice*, and
The Quiet American, to name only *my* favorites. He has had one
of the longest careers in film. In fact, the only other star—and

not exactly what we'd call a romantic hero—who wore spectacles previous to Caine was the silent film comedian Harold Lloyd, and his greatest films were made before Caine was even born.

Caine, with his hip, working man's Cockney accent and razor-sharp custom mohair suits from celebrity tailor Doug Hayward, seemed to give young men permission to be cool wearing glasses, and certainly a host of spectacle-wearing celebs, male and female, followed in his wake. Not to mention the celebrities who have used glasses as something of a personal style signature: Woody Allen, Yves St. Laurent, David Hockney, Anna Wintour, Andy Warhol, Johnny Depp, and Le Corbusier. Even Brad Pitt has been photographed wearing large, dark rectangular eyeglasses! (Try thinking of anything else those folks have in common.)

Many über-fashionable folks, on the other hand, prefer small, round frames, which are a suitable accessory for a variety of homespun, weathered looks: nerd chic, vintage chic, prairie chic, heritage chic, utility workers chic, and of course preppy chic. Funnily enough, this more capriciously retro approach in spectacles seems to runs parallel with its opposite style—and this is so often the case with spectacles—the rimless, titanium, supersonic, high tech, wraparound speedster variety, sleek as a new Porsche. In fact, if I'm not mistaken, there's a Porsche-brand of eyewear that fits that description.

It's all enough to make one wonder how opposite approaches like these can exist in fashion at the same time. I think what both backward- and forward-looking genres have in common in this case is a like-minded air of hyper-seriousness about them. The person of meaningful thought verses the person of determined action? Perhaps—but to truly understand this phenomenon, let's drop back a bit further than 1965. It's always a good thing to get our dates and facts straight at the beginning.

There seems to be agreement that the first treatise on optics was written by an Arabian astronomer and mathematician named Abu Ali al-Hasan ibn al-Haitham, known in the English-speaking world as Alhazen. His seven-volume *Treasury on Optics* was completed in Egypt in 1021 and came to be known in the West after it was translated into Latin in 1240. Alhazen's experiments were concerned with the properties of glass to make objects appear larger. This eventually led to glass and crystal balls being used as "reading stones" in the Middle Ages, a form of what later would be simply called a "magnifier."

By the end of the thirteenth century Venetian glass blowers were able to grind these stones into lenses and attached them to the face with wooden frames—so-called bridge frames, which were like today's eyeglasses but without the temple bars that hold the frames to the ears. Not that it mattered much in terms of reading books at the time, since most people were illiterate, but it became enormously important after 1455, when Johannes Gutenberg was first able to produce books using movable type, increasing the amount of reading matter available. Between that point and the sixteenth century, from England to China, spectacles evolved into common use. The first frames were simply tied to the face with ribbon, then side bars were substituted for the ribbon. The lorgnette—in effect, a frame with a handle—was designed by an Englishman named George Adams around 1780 and became popular during the Regency period, the heyday of the dandies. The monocle followed closely, as did spy and opera glasses (whose uses are reflected in the names).

Concurrent with these styles of eyewear were the increasingly popular "temple" sidebar spectacles, which by 1800 were being made in tortoiseshell, horn, silver, gold, brass, and nickel. The pince-nez also made an appearance about this time, but by the twentieth century the style we identify as modern today, temple spectacles, had won out.

Much of the 1900s was spent perfecting and complicating this design. By 1930 celluloid, the first thermoplastic synthetic to be manufactured, was being used for frame construction. In Germany, the Carl Zeiss Company developed the "perivist" spectacle, the frame shape we most recognize today: the temple arms were joined to the top of the front section, rather than the middle as was previously done. And then, in 1937, the American company Bausch & Lomb introduced the now-popular aviator shape, specifically designed for the fairly new profession of piloting airplanes.

Since that time each decade seems to have produced a signature shape. Or perhaps it would be better to say two antithetical signature shapes. Tortoiseshell glasses, sometimes known as horn rims—although both terms are misnomers because plastic has been used for years—became popular on university campuses in the 1940s and continued into the Ivy League '50s (see Chapter 14). These were invariably round or oval. But running counter to this were the heavy black plastic frames associated with Madison Avenue advertising executives (today think Woody Allen), which were rectangular.

By the time the Beatles invaded the United States in 1964 on a wave of Anglomania and screaming adolescent girls, the peacock revolution was in full swing: London's Carnaby Street, the Op Art movement, hippies, and Flower Power were all about to come into their own. Strongly architectural, futuristic Op Art school (picture early Elton John), and space suit eyewear were famously promoted by French designer André Courrèges. But the urban hip and the hippies were all wearing retro-look granny glasses like John Lennon and Janis Joplin—thin wire frames holding small ovals of tinted lenses. The maxis and the minis existed side by side, and they were soon joined by other varieties as well. By the early '70s designers were adding spectacles to their accessories lines with fun frames and sports eyewear.

The important recent developments have mostly been in technology. Polaroid sunglasses, with their polarizing filters to reduce UV rays, glare, and color distortion, were developed, and shock-resistant plastics have been invented; malleable titanium frames are popular for their lightweight comfort and durability.

I really didn't think much about spectacles until I was in my forties, and then it happened fast. It seemed that overnight I was

having problems with my near vision. I decided on frames rather than contact lenses for no other reason than that I'd put a positive spin on deteriorating eyesight and decided to use spectacles as another sartorial accessory: if you've got to join 'em, flaunt 'em. I found that glasses can be a wonderful pose in so many ways, actually enhancing the visual message you want to send about yourself to the rest of the world: playful, intelligent, serious, creative, well bred, even something of a renegade if that's what you want. You can jauntily take them off, twirl them in your hand, and affect a contemplative look, if the situation calls for it. An effective way to buy a few extra moments to figure out what the hell's going on.

At any rate, I was a fashion editor for *Town & Country* magazine at the time, and the taste in eyeglasses there was for very thin-rimmed tortoiseshell frames with round lenses. An old-school intellectual, preppy look that countered the heavier black and tortoiseshell frames being worn by the corporate world. The editor in chief at the time always wore a navy blazer, button down, and bow tie as well, to drive home the old-money, too-cool-to-care image. Since my background was university teaching, the style fell to me naturally—and stuck, because I've been wearing them ever since. I like to think of it as a sort of old-fashioned, dusty, professorial approach that coordinates easily with my love for porridge-thick tweed, old flannel, and rumpled linen. A low-keyed statement of the subtle ease and charm of tradition, a good mix of tat and chic. And amazingly enough, it actually seems to work very much in my favor. Sometimes I carry a few old books—hardcover of course, without dust jackets—around with me, anything faintly grubby and esoteric looking, to reinforce the impression that I'm studying something of mind-bending importance. I've found a satisfying form of one-upmanship is to rummage the index of one of them whenever someone takes out their latest high-tech device.

There are two schools of thought about signature eyewear accessories. One is that a person should stick to one style and use it perhaps more like a character trademark, a signature if you will (think David Hockney). The obvious strength in this approach is that it tends to send the signal that one is stable, secure, and not seduced into frivolous trends and fancies: A person, as the eighteenth century used to say, with solid bottom. A person with whom you might invest some money.

Of course, the downside of wearing only a single style of eyeglasses is that it's boring and predictable. Many have therefore opted for a wardrobe approach, using a different style for different moods and occasions, just as many folks have wardrobes of scents—using one cologne for day, another for evening; one in warm weather, another for cooler climes; that sort of thing. Sometimes a serious message wants to be sent, sometimes something more adventurous, carefree, and insouciant. As with any other grammar, in deciding on the right eyeglasses for your desired message, it helps to consider the occasion, the purpose, and the audience and adjust your approach accordingly.

In selecting eyewear, many people also treat the shape of the face as a determinate. I suspect this isn't quite as important as people think; indeed, using glasses to compensate for the peculiarities of one's face can lead to trouble, as overly large or small spectacles tend to be just too obvious and often therefore interpreted as an affectation, rather than something naturally accruing from a person's daily habits and culture.

Whether you want to enhance the natural shape of your face or play against it, the fundamental goal is to find frames that don't call attention to themselves. After all, the main purpose of dress is to make people concentrate on you, rather than on what you're wearing. To achieve this there are certain general rules: The front piece, regardless of shape, should be just short of the eyebrows on top, and just to the top of the cheek on bottom. Spectacles shouldn't be any wider than your face (this should seem obvious, but it's not). The bridge should fit well, certainly tight enough so that the glasses don't keep slipping down to the tip of your nose. These moderate parameters still allow for a number of shapes of aesthetic suitability.

And for those who are still considering contact lenses instead of spectacles, perhaps we should up-end Dorothy Parker's famous poem and consider it good advice:

> Women make passes
> *At men who wear glasses.*

11

FRAGRANCES

WHEN I WAS A BOY, as was the case for any male growing up in the middle of the twentieth century, the list
of fragrances for men basically consisted of barber shop items.
The only nonmedical balms ever applied to men was a splash
of witch hazel behind the ears and back of the neck by the barber (and these establishments were decidedly not hair styling salons). Real dudes might also ask for a drop of bay rum. These
two ointments, along with a liquid called Lilac Vegetal, a few
hair creams, and some talc, were all the scented products that
were available for men at the local drugstore, along with a few
aftershave splashes such as the ubiquitous Old Spice and Aqua
Velva. Anything more was considered suspect.

All that changed, of course, with the designer, youth, sexual,
and peacock revolutions of the mid-1960s, when men took up colognes and deodorants, scented shampoos and soaps, perfumed
shaving creams, hair sprays, moisturizers, body scrubs, and dozens of other products. Many of the items on this still-growing list
aim to condition, cleanse, restore, deodorize, color, smooth, and
protect our masculine skins and hair from the effects of the environment and aging, and to make us a bit more attractive—yet

most of them also possess some sort of scent that is intended
to enhance our smell. And too often, we simply slap the stuff
on without considering the fragrance with which we're anointing
ourselves.

It's worth noting that this growing list of grooming products—
and the men's retail space devoted to this is as large as it is for
women now, perhaps minus a few items of makeup—is based on
the psychological awareness by manufacturers that once we've
opened the door to dissatisfaction—that we don't look, smell, and
feel as good as we should—we've bought the whole ball of wax.
Statistics have indicated for some time now that neither cosmetics
nor surgical enhancement is any longer within the exclusive purview of women, just as gyms are no longer the men's clubs they
once were. We are now a unisex physical improvement culture.

I don't mean to give the impression that fragrances were the
exclusive purview of women before that point, because that
wouldn't be true. In classical Greece and Rome fragrance was
an integral part of social life for men rather than women; ancient Assyrian warriors curled their beards with scented oils; and
the Song of Solomon is chockablock with the most evocative and
erotic poetry about the sweet-smelling male lover, perhaps the
tamest passage of which is: "His cheeks are as a bed of spices,
as sweet as flowers; his lips like lilies, dropping sweet smelling
myrrh" (Song of Songs 5:13, Authorized KJV). An early example
of old spice.

In Medieval Europe both men and women used fragrances
to scent not only the body but the clothes and household fur-
nishings as well. In Renaissance times, bed coverings in aristocratic households were sprinkled with perfume and flower
petals, and linen chests were strewn with herbs and spices. Men
were known to douse their shirts with scented waters and oils.
Scented handkerchiefs were popular, as was the tactic of simply
stuffing the pockets with flower petals. Sometimes this was for a
somber purpose. The quatrain from this simple nursery rhyme,
for instance, is said to refer to the deadly Black Plague:

Ring-a-ring o'roses,
A pocket full of posies,
A-tishoo! A-tishoo!
We all fall down.

The explanation is that the first signs of contagion were rose-like rash rings appearing on the skin, and so flowers were carried to ward off the evil stench and hopefully prevent the disease from entering the body with the smell. It was all to no avail: sneezing and coughing would eventually indicate the coming of hemorrhaging, and the victim would fall dead. In truth, there's not enough evidence to support this interpretation; it remains a myth. We do know, however, that until germ theory gained traction in the nineteenth century, people thought diseases dwelt in the air and believed that scents could ward off these "miasmas."

It seems more likely that early lovers of fragrances took to them for the same reason we do: they smell good. First Italy and then France became renowned for its perfumes. Louis XIV was called "the sweetest smelling monarch that has been seen" and was so fond of perfume that he insisted on being in attendance while scents were being concocted to his own requirements by his perfumer. Court etiquette demanded that different scents be worn on different days of the week, and during Louis's reign Versailles became known as *la cour parfumée.*

In the eighteenth century gentlemen took to wearing cologne. This popular scent was originally known as *aqua admirabilis*, and it sprang into existence in the early 1700s, when two brothers, Johann Maria and Johann Baptiste Farina, decided to move their perfumery from Santa Maria Maggiore, Italy, to Cologne, Germany. Distilling essential oils (citrus such as lemons and oranges and herbs such as lavender, rosemary, and thyme) in alcohol diluted to a desired strength with some amount of water, they achieved considerable success with their scents, particularly when troops quartered in the city during the Seven Years War (1754–1763) bought copious supplies for themselves and to

send home. Thus it became known, as it has been ever since, as eau de cologne. Today the fragrance houses of Roger & Gallett and 4711 produce colognes that reflect the original scents.

Perhaps cologne's best-known advocate was Napoleon, who had a standing order with his perfumer for fifty bottles a month. He was a tad indulgent, but then emperors are expected to be. He indulged copiously and regularly, pouring a full bottle over himself after bathing and splashing another bottle or two on during the day whenever he felt the need to refresh himself. But the dandies, and a bit later their sartorial offspring, the "bucks" and "rakes" of the latter English Regency period, took fragrance-as-refreshment even a step further: they drank it as a pick-me-up after a taxing night on the town. Reading the various histories and diaries of the times, one might easily come to the conclusion that these hard-gambling, fast-driving friends of the prince regent—whose own perfume bills, by the way, usually amounted to about five hundred pounds a year, when a middle-class shopkeeper would have gotten along decently on an income of fifty pounds a year—would not have been above quaffing barrels of axle grease spiked with cat's urine. Cirrhosis of the liver must have killed off as many of the aristocracy as the Napoleonic Wars had.

It was just that sort of riotous living that tends to bring on sharp reaction, and when Victoria ascended the throne in 1837, the theme of "cleanliness is next to godliness" (even though those words were first preached by John Wesley in the 1750s) seemed to come with her. Ladies and gentlemen made a virtue of hot water and plenty of soap. In a speech he made at Aylesbury in 1865, Benjamin Disraeli, the queen's favorite prime minister, summed up the attitude: "Cleanliness and order are not matters of instinct; they are matters of education, and like most great things—mathematics and classics—you must cultivate a taste for them."

It was all part of the greater Victorian theme of discipline, in the wake of tremendously upsetting philosophical theories and scientific discoveries made by evolutionary biologists such as Charles Darwin and geologists such as Charles Lyell, who both greatly disturbed religious faith, not to mention the secular social philosophers such as Karl Marx and Friedrich Engels, Jeremy Bentham, John Stuart Mill, Herbert Spencer, and T. H. Huxley. (With attacks on belief coming from so many directions, it's no wonder Victorians were mad about regulation.)

The Regency dandy had disappeared from Bond Street, and the new gentleman, such as Victoria's consort, Prince Albert, remained in tactful ignorance of the potted and scented bottles of orris and patchouli. In reality he had merely retreated from these heavy scents to more subtle ones that accorded better with the idea of cleanliness. Lighter scents of lavender and verbena, orange and rose waters, and citrus fragrances were seen as a better complement to bathing. The man who affected strong perfumes, curled hair, and cosmetics—about which Regency bucks had little compunction or reserve—was thought to be not quite a gentleman.

It's taken us ever since then to transcend this attitude. It was, to name but one famous single instance, in the 1920s that screen idol Rudolph Valentino, an early-twentieth-century paragon of movie masculinity, was called an untoward name in print by a Chicago journalist, simply because the actor was known to wear cologne! Valentino actually went to Chicago and challenged the newsman to step into the ring with him, but the writer never showed.

We have now gotten over this puritanical aversion to scents on the male body. Fragrances are no longer considered the prerogative solely of women but are openly advertised by some of our more herculean athletes and virile actors, men who also curl, spray, and dye their hair and use depilatories, moisturizers, deodorants, bath oils, scented shaving creams, hand lotions, body scrubs, tanning gels, astringents, skin toners, sauna splashes, and genital sprays. Just like the rest of us. And the list keeps going. Hundreds of millions of dollars are spent on men's fragrances alone, never mind the rest of it. Some of these bouquets appeal to the more rugged among us and are packaged with ludicrous names: "Ammo," "Nose Tackle," "Saddle Sore," and "Rucksack," or something very much like that. Others take a more upscale approach, with names like "Eros," "Eau de Narcisse," and "Legend." Two of my favorite cologne names at the moment are "Spicebomb" (the bottle is actually shaped to resemble a World War II hand grenade) and "Arrogant," which you can't beat for chutzpah. (Should there not be several labeled "Old Money," "Divine Right," and "Your Royalness," or are they already on the market? Probably.)

Regardless of the packaging, fragrance is now an important aspect of male presentation—not only as a reflection of personal preference but also as an additional indicator of one's business image. Businessmen today are expected to have a varied wardrobe to see them through the various occasions of their lives and moods. After all, we've come to enjoy a growing diversity in our lives—yet many of us have not applied this diversity to our olfactory profile. There are still any number of men who doggedly stick to the barbershop basics or that callow cologne they first received as a teenage birthday gift.

Today there's an increased subtlety and sophistication about scents—a structure to them that we should all be aware of. There are scents more appropriate to the boardroom than the ballroom or bedroom; colognes more pleasing during the day than evening, winter than summer; and fragrances for moments of emotion rather than enterprise. If we consider a few simple rules and limit ourselves to a reasonable range of products, we can take care of most of our everyday fragrance needs.

As with clothing, men should really have a "wardrobe" of scents, so as to help them select one that's appropriate. Most men go about choosing a cologne from the toiletries bar by splashing a drop or two of several fragrances on the backs of their hands from bottles that either look appealing or have the name of a familiar designer brand on the label. They then go around sniffing themselves for the next half hour until they're totally confused and give up in frustration and go back to their old bottle of Bay Rum—or to one of the bottles that they received last holiday from the women in their lives and that, if used interchangeably, will last till the next holiday. This is decidedly a shame, for had they gone about selecting fragrances the right way, they'd have a nice collection by now, instead of the holiday assortment of fancy bottles about which we should be kind and say it's the thought that counts.

The better way is to first understand the basic terminology. Without getting all tangled up in the ornate chemistry involved, the fact is that the differences between fragrances are not much regulated by either the cosmetics industry or the government, nor is there a wealth of useful information on the labels. Generally though, from weakest to strongest, scents are labeled aftershave, cologne, toilet water, and perfume. This means that the essential oils responsible for the scent are concentrated more in perfume than in toilet water, for example, and the greater the concentration of these oils, the higher the price will be. Additionally, aftershaves may contain various emollients to lubricate the skin after having been scraped with a razor.

Second, know the various types of scents for gents: (1) citrus, derived from lemon, lime, grapefruit, orange, and bergamot; these scents are considered light and brisk with a fresh, summery quality; (2) spice, which generally includes nutmeg, cinnamon, clove, bay oil, and basil; these are considered heavier than citrus but still in the fresh category; (3) leather, usually concocted of the oils of juniper and birch, an aroma smoky rather than brisk; (4) lavender and various other florals, which are said to have a warm delicate scent; (5) fougère (French for fern-like), with a somewhat herbal green, outdoors scent; (6) woody, which includes vetiver, sandalwood, and cedar—all clean scented, but darker than fern; and (7) Eastern, such as musk, tabac, and some bay oils—these are the heaviest and most pungent.

These categories are unfortunately not as complete and precise as they should be, and for some time now science has attempted to devise a more universally accepted description to provide a more accurate way of categorizing scents. That prerogative remains by and large in the hands of the manufacturers, and thus something of an art dependent on the talents of expert sniffers, called in the trade "noses."

It's important to know the strength and type of scent because, in a business environment, a man should smell merely clean and fresh, not like a brothel in Marrakesh. Successful men are aware that the impression of cleanliness, with just a hint of sophistication thrown in for good measure, is all they need to make their presence known. Good fragrance doesn't overpower. So because heat tends to intensify fragrance, it's best to wear the lightest scents in warm weather and save the stronger ones for fall and

winter. Classic summer scents are of the citrus and fern varieties, which have a brisk, fresh, and bracing quality. Keeping a
bottle in a desk drawer as a refresher is a good idea in warm,
humid weather. Autumn and winter can better accommodate
the more redolent lavenders, leathers, and woodsy aromas. For
after-business hours a more definite fragrance can help establish
or enhance a mood of relaxation. The warmer scents of spice are
often a good choice here, and the richer Eastern ones. Both are
considered a bit romantic and linger longer. Social occasions also
allow us slightly more freedom to get away from the business
uniform and wear a more relaxing wardrobe, so why not also in-
dulge our scent wardrobe as well?

Like any wardrobe, your scent collection can get musty. Unlike some wines and people, scents don't improve with age, so
there's no point in saving or hoarding them. Use 'em, or lose 'em.
Even the best cologne will fade and change with time, particularly if exposed to direct sunlight, left unsealed, or subjected to
extremes in temperatures. All those holiday gift bottles will have
turned acrid by the time the new batch rolls in. This leads to
the economic thought that smaller bottles bought more often is a
better scheme than purchasing giant flagons. You're always sure
to have a fresh supply that way.

Experts tell us that scents react differently on different skins.
Always test the ones you're interested in before you buy. Having
a scent recommended to you is not enough. Splash a drop or two
on the inside of your wrist, rub your wrists together, and smell;
wait a few minutes, and smell again. If you still like the scent
the second time around—or in fact if the scent even remains
around for the second sniff—it's safe enough to buy. And don't
immediately try another scent. Wash your hands and wrists thoroughly, and wait a half hour before repeating this test with a new
cologne. Never try several at the same time because the olfactory
sense is both tenacious and perfectly capable of blending smells
together. By trying several scents at once, you'll have concocted

something entirely new, the results of which will be unpredictable. It's rather like mixing several drugs together—who knows what will happen?

On the other hand, when it comes to wearing cologne, don't limit yourself to the demure dab behind the ears either. Indeed, the very idea that there are prescribed places on the body for scents seems ludicrous. It's sometimes argued that anointing the pulse points is a good idea because that's where the heat is closest to the skin surface and provides greater impact to the fragrance. My feeling is that if you splash it around, you'll hit most of those points anyway. We don't have to be as lavish as Napoleon, but he does seem to have been on the right track.

12

GROOMING

IT'S THE AREA ABOVE THE SHOULDERS that calls for
the most attentive grooming: the neck, face, and head. Here,
as with the selection of fragrances (see Chapter 11), we can learn
from professionals—barbers, hair stylists, dermatologists, and
others schooled in the science of beauty.

The more technical aspects of grooming the face necessarily involve medical concerns. The correct way to shave; the best
shampoo for your hair and best moisturizer for your face; and
what to do about sun-damaged skin blemishes, wrinkles, hair
loss, acne, rashes, allergies, oily or dry skin, scarring, and a myriad of other concerns best left to medical science, which can give
us precise answers, advice, and information. Why should we rely
on advertising, as so many of us do, for our grooming advice?
Advertisers have always argued that one of their main functions
is to inform and educate; they say this without even smiling, the
wolves. But why rely solely on a thirty-second TV ad or a blurb
on a label as the ultimate educational tool?

The scientist of choice here is the dermatologist, whose purview is the physiology and pathology of the skin. Quite naturally, people think to consult a physician when they believe they

have a health problem, but physicians do and should serve another function as well. They can act as consultants in matters of
our daily regimens that touch directly on our health. Why not?
They've got the knowledge and study, and by advising us about
good grooming procedures and safe products, they'll save us from
health problems down the road.

While you should consult with a doctor in matters of grooming, you should also channel the artisan. Grooming, after all, en-
tails tools. There are tools for the hands—nail clippers, scissors,
file; the best tools for the face—tweezers, razor, and comb—are
the obvious basics in a good grooming kit. Scipio Africanus Minor (circa 185–129 BCE) would have been the first man in need
of a grooming kit, according to the Roman naturalist author Pliny
the Elder. He reports that Scipio was the first man he knew to
shave every day. And he traveled a great deal too, particularly in
North Africa and Spain.

A grooming kit isn't really necessary at home, since there
are so many places around the house in which to store these
requisites: in a medicine cabinet, drawer, or shelf, or even a
basket on a window ledge. But if we think in terms of a travel
grooming kit, we're sure to hit all the essential requirements.
Actually, I'd make that plural—kits. General travel packs—a
manicure kit, medical kit, and emergency packs—are what I
have in mind. It may sound a bit fussy at first, but talking with
frequent business travelers, I discovered that these packs can
be lightweight and compact, and provide a certain security
and peace of mind. General grooming kits come in a variety
of shapes and sizes, from the Dopp style, with its elongated
shape and zipper down the middle, to rolls and bags. Some are
made of high quality leather, others of cotton canvas or nylon
or other synthetic fabrics. While some have a preference for
luxury here, and others opt for the convenience of the lightest
weight, what makes the most sense is that, whatever style you
choose, the kit should have a liquid-resistant lining and enough
compartments to keep items separated.

For a general grooming kit, apart from cologne, deodorant, and shampoo, you'll need shaving and tooth care paraphernalia. Razors are electric (either plug-in or battery), safety (with one or more blades), or straight. Although straight razors (with a long single blade and some sort of a handle) were the only razors used for two thousand years—bronze and iron ones were common in first-century Rome—they are almost unheard of today. The few men who use them may enjoy a nostalgic reverie of Edwardian times, when gentlemen wore celluloid collars, dabbed their hair with Macassar oil, and lathered up by whipping their shaving soap in a porcelain bowl and applying it with an ivory-handled beaver brush, and swear there's no better shave. But straight razors are both difficult to use and dangerous—they weren't called "cutthroats" for nothing—since it's merely the practiced precision of the hand that prevents serious cuts. These razors also need constant attention to sharpening, called "stropping," after the name of the leather belt used for that purpose—something we moderns can do without, unless you want to add another thankless chore to your daily routine.

Contemporary preference is for the electric or single-edged safety razor. Neither can inflict serious cutting damage because the blade isn't exposed enough to do more than cut the hair—and occasionally nick the skin, but this tends to happen only when we're in a hurry or have an important meeting. The safety razor was first patented in the 1880s, but it was a man named King Camp Gillette who patented the first popular safety razor in 1901; the small, double-edged model stayed in fashion for the next half century. Men who were old enough to have used straight razors remembered King Gillette in their prayers ever after. Today throwaway plastic safety razors with multiple blades can be bought in packs costing just a few dollars, or in more exotic materials (silver or gold, chrome, pewter, staghorn, rare woods, bone, ceramic, and almost anything else you can think of) with considerably heavier price tags. No matter what type of handle you prefer, each of these razors will take virtually the same blades and give the same quality shave, making the matter of price solely an aesthetic concern rather than a utilitarian one.

Electric razors are found in a variety of styles designated by the design of the head, whether they must be plugged into an electric outlet or are battery powered (or both, and batteries are either rechargeable or replaceable). Most are either foil-headed, in which the blades move back and forth under a thin metal shield, or rotary-headed, with rotating blades covered with spring-mounted guards. There is an incredible variety of these shavers to suit a wide range of faces and needs, some rather large, heavy, and powerful and others small, light, and compact. Often the best advice about these tools can be found in what are called beauty supply houses, places where hair stylists and other professionals buy their products.

Shaving soaps are found in pots, tubes, and cans. Potted soaps (usually in ceramic jars or wooden bowls with replaceable rounds of soap) are applied with a shaving brush, and while the soap is competitively priced, a good shaving brush can be an expensive investment. Cheap brushes wear out quickly and are not as soft on the skin even when new. The best brushes are made of badger hair, unbeatable for comfort and longevity. Small tubes of shave cream are good for travel, but most men use canned gels at home as both the most economical and practical. All shave soaps come in a wide range of scents (or fragrance free), but the cans seem to have the greatest variety of formulations: "For Tough Beards," "Sensitive Skin," "Medicated," and the like, although most of the ingredients listed on the labels are pretty much the same.

Last among the list of basic shaving gear is the lowly styptic pencil or alum block. Found in every drugstore, this handy device is the time-proven way to staunch the flow of blood aside from cauterization. It's an astringent made of alum with a quick hemostatic ability to contract the skin tissue and blood vessels. Alum has been used as a styptic since at least the fifteenth century, and what men's shirt collars looked like before this ingenious tool was discovered doesn't bear thinking about. It's child's play to use: just wet the tip, rub it back and forth across the nick, allow to dry to a film of white powder, and wipe away the residue. There's a tiny ouch at the beginning, but I like to think that's put in purposefully, for character building.

There are also a number of products having to do with the pre- and post-shaving experience. Balms, astringents, and moisturizers all profess assisting the shave and promoting healthier skin. We should be aware of these products, but ask professionals if they're indeed necessary or advisable—and, if so, which brands might be best for our particular types of skin and lifestyles.

Other grooming tools should be kept in a separate manicure kit, and that's often the way they're sold. The basic implements are nail scissors, clipper, nail file, tweezers; additions may include emery board (which is really just a very fine filing device) and orange stick (funnily enough a stick traditionally made of orange wood used to push the cuticle back from the nail), and

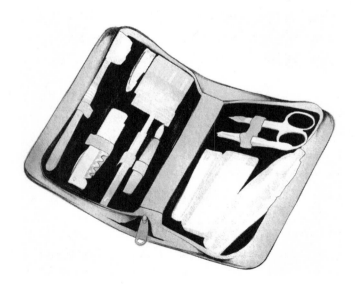

additionally sized scissors or clippers as needed. Perhaps a small
mirror, a small Swiss army knife, and a comb. Some firms specialize in these tools and stock literally dozens of different shapes
and sizes of each implement to satisfy every grooming require-
ment, including such things as loofahs, pumice bars and callus
removers, battery-powered trimmers, and more specialized and
esoteric items.

Kits to hold medications can be found in pharmacies as well.
These are usually lined with waterproof fabric and contain vials
for pills and vitamins, bottles for liquids, a folding spoon, ther-
mometer, and occasionally other health-related items such as
contact-lens container, swabs and adhesive bandages, and basic
first aid pack. They're a good, simple way to keep medical needs
handy. When packing them, consider the following tips: (1) retain a checklist of medications as well as extra prescriptions, just
in case any necessary meds you're carrying go missing and need
to be refilled while you're away from home; (2) label all vials and
bottles; (3) always keep the medical kit with carry-on luggage,
never in checked baggage; and (4) know the expiration date of all
medications, and restock as necessary.

These medical kits are better for some things than for others;
they will probably not do you much good if the Richter scale hits
7.5 or if you're in the direct path of a tsunami, but they can come
in handy if you're stranded at an airport or have to reschedule a
flight, or experience any number of those other maddening little
accidents that befall every traveler from time to time. The main
thing to remember with them, and with grooming in general, is
this: you want to be presentable when you arrive, no matter what
time you get there.

And speaking of being presentable, it's worth noting that the
actual quantity and cut of facial hair—once the subject of intense regulation and scrutiny—is these days more a matter of
personal choice and professional decorum than anything else.
The subject of facial hair was for many years well understood:
there wasn't any. From just after World War I to the 1960s, the

"business look" prescribed a clean-shaven face. Occasionally a man might try a mustache (think of film star Clark Gable for example), but beards of any sort were thought bohemian, the sort of thing you'd only see in New York's Greenwich Village on Beatniks in the 1950s (think poet Allen Ginsberg, for example).

We've loosened up a great deal since those restrictive days, and both beards and mustaches are a popular alternative to being clean-shaven. Anything from a bit of stubble to a full-grown "lumberjack" covering is perfectly acceptable. Most men experiment at least once in their lives with facial hair. The style of a mustache and beard is a decidedly individual choice, a matter of personal flair and what the wearer wants to convey about himself. A very close-shaven growth tends to indicate a nonchalant urbanity, while a full and long beard makes us think of rural wilds and rustic lifestyles. And these are merely associations from past experiences and examples; there really are no hard and fast rules about this sort of thing, no sweeping aesthetic or moral imperative. Just as there is a general rule about the size of shirt collars—that they should be in proportion to the size of the face—there is a basic admonition about facial hair: the mustache or beard should be in relative proportion to the size of the face. A long, thin face wearing a wide, thick mustache or large beard tends to make the hair look as if it has a life of its own—which means that the detail gets noticed rather than you.

The only other cautionary advice worth giving is that an unkempt, dirty beard or mustache, regardless of its style and volume, is not a pleasantry for viewers. Whatever style a man chooses, he should trim his growth regularly and keep it clean (eating can present problems to be habitually addressed), because slovenliness without oft proclaims slovenliness within. Buy the appropriate grooming tools for the job: there are a whole range of grooming aids in this area, from mustache waxes to beard oils and clippers, but a good mustache scissors, comb, and beard trimmer are essential. And use them daily.

13

ITALIAN STYLE

ANY BOOK ABOUT MEN'S FASHION today must pay attention to the clothes of Italy, both because the Italians control the high end of the market in manufacturing and textiles, and because their custom tailors are internationally famous. "The fine Italian hand," as it has often been called, is the work of the true artisan and the craftsmanship of those makers of distinction, that handful of small firms devoted to dressing the gentleman in masterpieces of sartorial artistry, individual creations of incomparable skill, taste, and propriety, which are less and less found in a world increasingly dominated by shoddy workmanship and grubby conformity. As we drown in online streaming, microwaved meals, and touchscreens galore, true craftsmanship is more and more in demand as the last luxury.

The Italian sense of style is hardly to be argued. Whether in furniture, sports cars, architecture, kitchen utensils, or clothes, the Italians have made their mark. And it has been said that style is what Italy is all about. Italians nurture it, cultivate it, wallow in it, and of course, export it.

Why are fashion and style so well understood in Italy? Perhaps it's because the Italian wants to dress well. He is an individualist, after all; he wants to be seen as his own man, and he understands the role of clothing in helping him to reach that goal. The frequently echoed sentiment, usually attributed to the twentieth-century Calabrian writer Corrado Alvaro, is that "once Italian humanity is lost, everything is lost," and one can tease out the implications for style.

Italy seems always to have had a stylistic edge. Even that most cynical of travelers, Mark Twain, said during a voyage he made to Europe and the Holy Land in 1867 that the Creator had made Italy from designs by Michelangelo. Today, despite whatever political and economic turmoil there may be, the artistic flowering of Italy continues, and the influence is felt. Its filmmakers, from Vittorio De Sica and Federico Fellini to Franco Zeffirelli and Lina Wertmüller, continue to chart new courses in cinema; architects, such as the pioneering Pier Luigi Nervi with his "bravura" style in concrete, have revolutionized contemporary building and the urban landscape. Italians have surpassed the Scandinavians in sleek furniture and interior design and rivaled the French in haute couture. And who has created more beautiful automobiles, printed silks, or sculpture?

While other nations—the great scientific and technological empires with their staggering economic engines—seek their destiny on the grand scale, policing the world, measuring the galaxies, and generally deciding the fate of the universe, Italy goes about its time-honored way of providing personal and intimate pleasures, catering to those who seek an elegant pair of shoes or a noble glass of wine rather than the latest microcomputer, fastest particle accelerator, or most destructive ICBM. Not to say that superconductors, the Higgs boson, and missile-launching drones aren't important, perhaps even more so than a handmade linen shirt—but which touches us more closely?

Not that we should be so narrow as to be concerned with only what touches us directly, but we should care about the fate of these things. Italy seems more a haven and refuge for those human concerns, those small, daily, direct pleasures that are so much in rapid decline elsewhere. This concern for the individual, for the more personal triumphs that craftsmanship bestows, is really a part of a larger aesthetic sense. The relationship between craftsmanship and an appreciation for beauty is a product of Italian culture. And culturally, it has been said, we are all Italy's children. Indeed the influence of Italy, its people, and its culture on the rest of Europe, on the world, is the subject of dozens of university courses, thousands of art lectures, and innumerable books (some scholarly, some humorous, some both). In the arts and sciences, in commerce, exploration, politics, philosophy, and a host of lesser pleasures, Italy has been pivotal. One of those pleasures is fashion.

Historically, Italy has been the great bridge, the delicate balance between Northern Europe and the Middle East, sensitive to the pressures of France, Germany, Scandinavia, and Britain as well as Greece, Turkey, and the farthest reaches of Asia. As early as the thirteenth century one could have seen in the thriving port of Venice cargo ships from every trading nation in the known world. While London was still a walled medieval town of dark, narrow alleys, Venice had already reached its height of prosperity, a city of sumptuous palaces, gold mosaic churches, and spacious, sculpture-filled piazzas. Northern Europe was built of brick and stone; Italy of marble.

Even during the Middle Ages, because of the extraordinary geographical position and political influence and wealth of Italy, the Italians became the great merchants, bankers, and traders in Europe—and their fashion industry boomed accordingly. Silk, that regal fabric so much in demand in the aristocratic households of Europe after the fifteenth century, had been woven at Palermo since 1148. By the fifteenth century Italy had already developed extensive production techniques for both silk and wool, international trading networks, and a modern banking system, all of which were reflected in the enormous mercantile wealth of Genoa, Venice, Florence, and Milan. By the mid-seventeenth century the Barberis Canonico family—now known

as Vitale Barberis Canonico, the largest woolens mill in Italy—
was already involved in textile manufacture.

Tailoring as we know it—like almost everything else as we
know it—began with the Renaissance, whose history is inextri-
cable from that of Italy. Actually, cutting and tailoring—the two
basic aspects of the craft of constructing clothes from patterns—
began to develop gradually in the eleventh century. According to
the scholar Carole Collier Frick, in *Dressing Renaissance Florence: Families, Fortunes, and Fine Clothing*, "The earliest mention specifically of a tailor in Florence comes from the year 1032,
noting the physical location of a shop, 'Casa Florentii Sarti.'"
While in Milan, a *corporazione* of weavers, tailors, and dyers to
make clothing existed as early as 1102. The *Oxford English Dictionary*'s first reference to the word "tailor" gives the specific date
of 1297, and the Geneva Bible, with its famously amusing trans-
lation of Genesis 3:7—"They sewed figge tree leaves together,
and made themselves breeches"—wasn't published until 1560,
by which time the ideas of tailoring had obviously already taken
firm hold throughout Europe.

Tailoring was shaped by what has come to be known as Humanism: a broad, deep concern for the human, for the personal
and social life in this world as opposed to the spiritual concerns
of life in the next. The difference between the emphasis on the
otherworldly in the Middle Ages and the worldly concerns of the
Renaissance can easily be discerned in the dress of the two periods. Contrast the Gothic miniatures, for example, with fifteenth-
century portraits, Giotto's *Lamentation* (circa 1305) with Jan
Van Eyck's *Giovanni Arnolfini and His Bride* (circa 1434). Little
more than a hundred years separate these two paintings, but the
differences are immense. More often than not, human figures
in medieval paintings like *Lamentation* look as though they are
wearing long sheets of stiff foil, coverings that give little indication of the body's shape beneath. Renaissance portraits such
as *Giovanni Arnolfini and His Bride*, on the other hand, seem to
exult in individuality and corporeality.

During the Middle Ages clothing was regarded as a means of concealing the body; it was not until the guild systems of the late Middle Ages that there was even any differentiation between clerical and secular dress. With the rise of Humanism, however, came the accentuation, even the glorification of the human form. This is our basis for fashion.

It might be possible to define this fashion revolution as the steady process of corporeal revelation through clothing. The loose robe, the standard uniform of the medieval period, was shortened and tightened, and eventually cut and pieced together in attempts to approach the idealized contours of the human body. These attempts began to call for expert skill and division of labor.

This was the moment when the cutter and the tailor joined other craftsmen as important members of the artisanal community. Until this time, all but the most aristocratic Europeans made their own clothes, from simple woven cloth stitched together and draped over the body. The weaver produced the cloth, the distinguishing feature of this type of clothing. More and more after 1300, however, the tailor took on equal importance with the weaver. Guilds at this time specialized in various crafts, and a variety of guilds sprang up to assume responsibility for dressing the Renaissance gentleman: doublet makers, belt and sash makers, furriers, weavers and dyers, embroiderers and the like, each skill jealously guarded by the guild membership.

The rise of the tailor parallels the rise of the cities in Europe. Master tailors were charged with clothing residents of the continent's growing towns, and so the art and science of tailoring became a highly specialized, complex, and jealously guarded craft. This first happened in Italy.

Italian fashion in the Renaissance period was characterized by intricately decorated, delicate, and sumptuous fabric. There was a heightened concern for appearance since the Italian cities had become world stages for the great dramas of life in a modern world. Luigi Barzini, in his classic book *The Italians*, notes that a reliance on symbols and spectacles is a fundamental trait of the national character:

> It is, incidentally, one of the reasons why the Italians have always excelled in all activities in which appearance is predominant: architecture, decoration, landscape gardening, the figurative arts, pageantry, fireworks, ceremonies, opera, and now industrial design, jewelry, fashion, and the cinema. Italian medieval armor was the most beautiful in Europe: it was highly decorated, elegantly shaped, well designed, but too light and thin to be used in combat. The Italians themselves preferred the German armor, which was ugly but practical. It was safer.

One can conjecture that appearances become more important in a culture as the culture itself becomes more public—as, for example, city architecture presents more of a public stage for the dramas of daily life. And public stages seem to work better in warmer climates. The Englishman says his home is his castle, and he has his private clubs for social life. But the Italian lives in the world of the cafe and the piazza; he spends more time in public places, which explains the great beauty of the town square in Italy. I believe it was Stendhal, the noted French novelist (who lived the last twenty-eight years of his life in Milan), who said that "only a total lack of decency could keep one from joining the daily *corso*." Even the dour New Englander Nathaniel Hawthorne reacted favorably to Italian street life, writing, "I never heard from human lips anything like this bustle and babble, this thousand-fold talk that you hear about you in the crowd of a public square; so entirely different it is from the dullness of a crowd in England, where . . . hardly a dozen monosyllables will come from the lips of a thousand people." This concept of the street as a *salone del popolo*, the people's parlor, makes every *via* a stage, a place to see and be seen, to confirm one's status in the community in the best possible light.

Climate, to be sure, has made the difference in other regards as well. The Mediterranean has given the Italians sunshine and warmth and vibrant color. These, in turn, produce a heightened sense of the visual, a more acute sense of the physical environment, with its intricate and subtle beauty. This aesthetic sense inevitably manifests itself in what Italians create. And certainly Italy has an abundance of natural and created beauty. Lord Byron, that inexhaustible lover of life who spent his last days wandering in Italy, penned an appropriate tribute: "Italia, oh, Italia! Thou who hast / The fatal gift of beauty."

Italy's long tradition of man-made beauty found even greater expression in the twentieth century than it did in the Renaissance. The modern history of Italian men's fashion begins at a fashion show held at the Grand Hotel in Florence in January 1952. The great impresario of Italian fashion Giovanni Battista Giorgini had been staging women's fashion shows in the Sala Bianca of Palazzo Pitti, but for the January '52 show he added male models to accompany the female models down the runway. Brioni of Rome, the tailoring firm started by Nazareno Fonticoli and Gaetano Savini immediately after the liberation of the city in 1945, presented a number of colorful silk shantung tuxedos for the male models to wear as they accompanied the female models.

It was the first time menswear was seen on a fashion runway. The famous Manhattan department store B. Altman decided to buy the Brioni collection as well as the women's wear. By 1954, Brioni had crossed the Atlantic and held its first fashion show in New York, and the rest is history. Men's clothing had entered the realm of fashion.

Brioni was and is centered in Rome, but what makes Italy unique is that several areas of the country lay claim to schools of tailoring, and each one has its own unique style. Considering the tailoring from north to south, there are the Milanese, the Florentines, the Romans, and the Neapolitans. It was the Romans who made the initial impact, but in the development of postwar manufacturing, attention focused on the industrially and technologically advanced North and its capital, Milan. After all, the North was the traditional home of silk and woolens textile production.

To be sure, there were great menswear designers farther south in Italy, but money and quality manufacturing seemed to flow northwards. From the late 1950s up through the '70s, Carlo Palazzi and Bruno Piattelli were making headlines for their sophisticated collections in Rome, and the tailoring houses of Rubinacci and Attolini in Naples were renowned. Beginning in the 1960s, however, the name to be reckoned with would be a designer from Piacenza: Giorgio Armani.

It's always been my contention that Armani would be historically better known for his menswear designs than his women's wear. After deciding against a career in medicine, Armani took a job as a menswear buyer with the Milan department store La Rinascente in 1954, which led to his eventual branching out as a house designer for a variety of Italian labels, predominantly with the Cerruti group in the 1960s, before starting his own label in 1974. His substantial legacy was secured during this period and the decade that followed, with his successful attempt to soften men's tailored clothing. There have been many words used in the fashion press to describe this—"deformalization," "sensualization," "deconstructualization," and even "feminization"—all of them true enough. The important point is that this shift, whatever we call it, changed the way we think about the cut of the modern suit.

Deconstruction must have been on Armani's mind for a long time when he designed his own collection, because he immediately set about eviscerating the tailored coat—in both the suit and the sports jacket. In doing so, Armani changed the way men dressed.

Armani purposefully altered the business wardrobe. He made the English sports jacket more comfortable by taking out much of the stiff padding and interlinings, using softer and more highly textured fabrics, and enlarging the silhouette slightly by dropping and broadening the shoulders, lowering the lapel gorge and button stance, and slightly lengthening the jacket. The jacket began to ease, to purposefully sag a bit, to look broken in, like it had been worn for years right off the rack—in essence, to look *sensual*.

Armani's vision came to fruition in the 1980s and made him arguably the most important name in menswear as an innovative designer: no other designer had changed the silhouette and fabrics of men's tailored clothing as he had. His tailored collection was now filled with soft suits and jackets made from traditional women's wear fabrics such as wool bouclés and crepes, high-twist yarns, superfine twills, velvets, lightweight lambswool and cashmeres, all in muted palettes of dusty tan and mossy olive, foggy grays, faded plums, pewter, and tobacco brown. He experimented with drape cutting (as the English themselves had done in the early 1930s), allowing small amounts of superfluous fabric in the chest and shoulders and back, which produced a slightly corrugated ripple of fabric across the upper front and back of the coat. Sleeves were minimally widened, and side pockets minimally lowered.

It was a bold reinvention of business dress for the modern man, a looser, softer, more romantic look in tailored clothing, and Armani remained faithful to it until the summer of 1994, when he introduced his Nuova Forma collection, in which he returned to a more shaped and slightly more constructed jacket. But his reputation is secure. Comfort in tailoring, sophisticated and finely tuned coordination of colors, and an emphasis on softness in construction and fabrics created a new international style for a new international man—all of this can be attributed to Armani. The stiff, heavy, dark, highly structured Victorian business suit was finally dead and buried. And for this liberating revolution, he will be remembered with gratitude by everyone designing men's clothing today, not to mention their customers. The movement toward comfort has been one of the great forces in modern clothing, and Armani has played a very large part in that story. There is a direct line from him to the lightweight clothing we wear today.

This new emphasis on softness and comfort inevitably turned attention to the tailors of Naples, who had begun experimenting with deconstruction in the 1930s. Indeed it's odd that it took Armani, a Milanese designer, to present this approach to the world in the 1960s because it was exactly what the Neapolitan tailors Gennaro Rubinacci and Vincenzo Attolini had done thirty years before. Had Armani been aware of these early experiments done in the South before the war? In any case, by the 1980s the names of Rubinacci, Attolini, and Kiton began to be seen in better men's shops in the United States.

At first, American men didn't quite know what to make of this sort of jacket, with its natural, rounded shoulders and shallow chest, its full sleeve head, shorter length, front darts that went from mid-chest to hem, and unlined interior. Giorgio Armani had produced a more comfortable jacket by enlarging the silhouette and using softer fabrics. The Neapolitans, masters of tailoring that they are, were more interested in *deconstructing* the garment to achieve comfort. They removed the heavy infrastructure to produce a mere shell of a coat. As soon as American men put it on they noticed its lightness and easy gracefulness, because the Neapolitan tailors had in great measure achieved the ideal: a jacket that was lightweight and comfortable, but still had shape.

Heritage had played a part here. The Neapolitans were very much aware of the traditional English silhouette—Naples had been a stop on the English Grand Tour for centuries—and appreciated the subtle shape of the English coat. After all, hadn't Gennaro Rubinacci, one of the most famous tailoring firms in the city, called his business London House in tribute to English style? But of course British fabrics and heavy padding would never do in the heat and humidity of the Mediterranean. And so the Neapolitan artisans set about to "improve" the construction. Opening the sleeve and making it more flexible, shaping the chest and skirt of the jacket with a longer dart so that padding was superfluous, stitching the shoulder to overlap the sleeve head so no shoulder pads were necessary, and using half linings rather than full ones. The jacket seems slimmer from the outside but actually feels looser from the inside.

These tailors were used to working with lighter-weight fabrics such as silk and linen, fine cottons and tropical-weight worsteds. But unlike Armani thirty years later, who would use high technology and enlarged silhouettes to achieve comfort, these tailors put considerable handwork into the construction, fashioning each seam with special techniques that made the jacket lighter, more supple, airier. In the end, the answer to the high technology of the North was the low technology of the South. The factories of Northern Italy are immaculate fields of buzzing machinery; in the South, the factories are quiet tables around which men and women sew in their laps. This organized production of artisans is referred to as "island" manufacturing.

Unsurprisingly, it's said that there are more tailors in the vicinity of Naples than anywhere else on earth. These artisans have now come into their own, and rightly so. By devising "factories of tailors" as a production method, they have figured out a way to bring Old World craftsmanship into the twenty-first century. We should all be grateful.

Today the Italian look is defined by a sophisticated forwardness of styling. The Italians prefer to lead, rather than follow fashion. The *bella figura* tends toward a less constructed garment in lighter-weight fabrics—Italian tailors are masters with linens, silks, and cottons. In the North, where the weather is cooler, dress is a bit more conservative, and the business uniform is for navy blue suits, dark brown silk ties (did the Milanese invent the

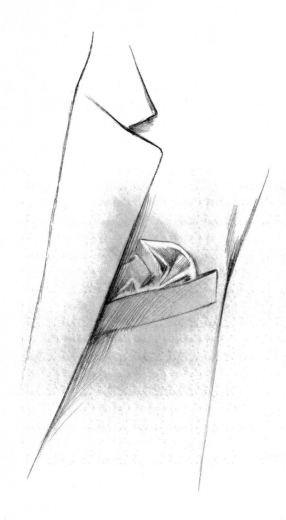

eye-catching color combination of blue and brown?), and white shirts. And brown shoes, because Italians consider black shoes both funereal and uninteresting.

In the South, the Neapolitans have developed their own idiosyncrasies in the details. Pockets are a special pleasure, and one sees patch pockets in the unique "brandy glass" shape—with the bottom of the pocket wider than the top and rounded—on both suits and sports jackets. There's also the famous *barchetta* chest pocket, which is curved into the chest of the jacket and resembles the little boat for which it's named.

The sleeve head of the coat, rather than being smooth, is pleated because the Neapolitan tailors like a large top sleeve set into a small shoulder hole. To achieve this effect they use what's called a "closed" construction method, in which the sleeve and shoulder fabric is overlaid without benefit of heavy padding; it makes for a lighter, more flexible jacket. And the front seams of the coat, the darts, are usually extended all the way down from the mid-chest to the hem of the garment. It's considered a better way of controlling the shape of the garment below the side pockets (called by tailors the "skirt").

Today, as in previous eras, the farther south one goes in Italy, the more color plays a part in the wardrobe, presumably because the weather becomes warmer and sunnier. Much of this also has to do with a more casual lifestyle that accompanies lemon and orange trees, the dazzling blue of the Mediterranean, red tile roofs, and the incessant blur of motor scooters. Comfort, color, and construction rule here. Men's clothing has been trending in this direction for the past century, and the future seems likely to be no different.

And just as the English have a long tradition of wearing their country clothes to town, Italian men have a penchant for mixing the playful with the serious when putting together an outfit. A somber suit is often matched with a patterned shirt and colorful tie, bright socks often peek out from under discreet trousers, or a vibrant pocket square from the breast pocket of an otherwise sedate coat. It's particularly noticeable that Italian men seem to have a decided aversion to black shoes and prefer brown ones with every outfit. An Italian friend of mine once explained this to me by noting that black shoes are merely black, while brown can run an almost infinite range of shades from the lightest cream or biscuit to taupe, fawn, mahogany, chestnut, chocolate, espresso, and sable. "It's so much more interesting, don't you think?" he mused. I couldn't but agree, but then any black clothing puts me off.

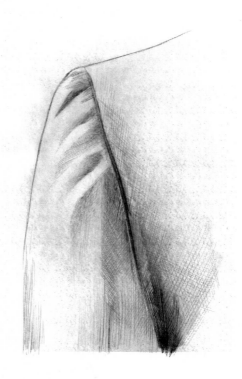

14

IVY STYLE

WHEN I WAS GROWING UP in the late 1950s, the matter of dress for young, middle-class men was relatively simple. When a boy reached adolescence, he would put away much of his childhood wardrobe—whatever that might have been—and, if he were thinking about college, begin to put together a basic outfit that would see him through those coming years and beyond. It was a time before the designer revolution in menswear, before the Laurens and Armanis, the Thom Brownes and Dolce & Gabbanas, and everyone else who wanted to get in on the act. It was a time of known shops and branded manufacturers. Tradition still seemed to be a body of beliefs, rather than merely a commodity to be exploited.

In the mid-twentieth century United States, there were basically three types of men's clothing stores. There was the men's store for the American business look: conservatively cut suits in either plain or striped worsteds, safe shirts (the majority of which were white, with a medium point collar), and discreet foulard neckwear. Men who wore this look wore plain black oxfords and plain dark socks. Dark gray felt fedoras were still seen in sizeable numbers.

Then there was the more modish store, a classier version of the trad businessman's enclave, a bit more upscale, hipper, more for the man who was known for caring about style. In the late '50s this store took on a bit of European flair: the suits had a "Continental" cut (meaning Italian) or British look. The fabrics were different here—more gabardines, mohairs, flannels, and silks than worsteds, and with more pattern selection. At these stores you could find silk knit neck ties and shirts in slightly bolder stripes, cashmere sweater vests, and Burberry trench coats.

And then there were the Ivy League shops.

The period 1945 to 1965 was the golden age of the classic "campus shops," stores that had built a reputation for catering to the sartorial needs of those with EEE (Eastern Establishment Elite) aspirations, *adresses d'or* such as J. Press, the Andover Shop, Langrock, Chipp, and Brooks Brothers. These wonderful clothiers were first situated in the cities and towns where the great universities were located: Harvard, Princeton, Yale, and the other Ivy League schools. By the early 1950s they had spread far and wide: virtually every city and college town had a campus shop catering to the style of the students, all supplied by US manufacturers, bolstered by a contingent of British imports.

The golden age of Ivy League can be dated from the end of World War II to Woodstock. It began with the passage of the Servicemen's Readjustment Act, popularly known as the G.I. Bill, in 1944. This was the act of Congress that allowed so many young ex-servicemen (and women) loans to buy houses, start businesses, and most importantly attend colleges and universities. It's been estimated that by the time the original program ended in 1956, as many as 2.2 million men and women had used the bill for higher education benefits; some statistics indicate higher education enrollment increased tenfold in the decade from 1945 to 1955.

In another decade the Ivy style trend would start to wane as the military draft grew, and many students—the majority of whom were no longer EEE types, or even aspirants to that clan—took to the hippie style of the New Left. Ivy style moved further and further to the political right. Richard Nixon dressed in Brooks Brothers suits, after all. Little wonder that, in footage of Woodstock, the dominant mode of dress seems to have been nudity.

During its heyday, however, the Ivy League look was a blessing for the young men—often of growing middle-class means and aspirations—who attended these institutions of higher learning in greater and greater numbers. They found that they could construct a basic campus wardrobe without a lot of money or effort. There was a high serviceability and low maintenance to the college wardrobe of the day.

The basic items were the oxford button-down shirt and cotton khaki trousers. Khaki cotton cloth had been used for hundreds of thousands of uniforms during both World War II and the Korean War, and army-navy stores sprouted up everywhere to sell off the surplus. In cooler weather, a Shetland crewneck sweater in any color was added. A pair of brown penny loafers and white tennis shoes (or white or tan bucks, or boating moccasins) constituted an acceptable range of footwear. For outerwear, a cotton gabardine balmacaan raincoat (always tan) and a stout duffel coat (always either tan or navy) were all that were needed, although many a young man also had a cotton "Baracuta" golf jacket (also tan). A tweed sports jacket (Harris or Shetland) or a navy single-breasted blazer was favored for semi-dress attire, and a gray flannel suit for dress. Summer semi-formality was assured with a seersucker or tan poplin suit; some of the more assured students had madras sports jackets. For more formal occasions, a plain dark gray tropical worsted suit always worked (the trousers would also be worn with the sports jackets). A half-dozen ties (rep-striped regimentals, foulards, or clubs) and the necessary complement of underwear, socks, pajamas, and handkerchiefs filled out the basics.

If the clothes were properly fitted, of an acceptable cut and styling, and made well, these items would do a young man proud no matter where he was going or on what occasion, from a meeting with his academic adviser to a faculty tea, classy campus dance, or job interview. And while the wardrobe itself was relatively simple, there were intricacies of cut and quality to these basic items that belied their straightforwardness. The true Ivy-style sports jacket, for instance, is characterized and distinguished by a detailed quarter-inch stitching along the edge of the lapels (and sometimes the edge of the collar, pocket flaps, and seams as well). It's a tellingly sporty touch—and it's little details like these, nuances that are so obscure, so overlooked by the novice, that are so tellingly important for the aficionado. That knowledge, furthermore, is really what separates the members of the club from those who merely wear clothes. As novelist of the EEE Louis Auchincloss pointed out in one of his novels (it must have been *Manhattan Monologues,* since that's the last one I've read), "To the untutored eye all the horses look alike from the stands, and sometimes even to the tutored."

Good jackets were always three-button and natural-shouldered, softly constructed in the chest and cut on the easy side without darts. They were generically called "sack" coats because they weren't shaped in the waist and they hung straight down from the shoulders. Lapels extended about a third of the way across the chest, and true believers were quick to point out that the rear of the jacket must have a "hook" vent, that is, a center vent with a one-inch folded-over seam at the top.

Trousers were cut easy too, trim but roomy, just this side of baggy. These were cuffless and pleatless, otherwise unadorned, and worn with a variety of belts. (Braces, or suspenders, were in the 1950s for dinosaurs, the insecure, or the extremely affected). Everything, needless to say, shouldn't look new, shiny, or stiff. Quality meant longevity: raincoats, khakis, tweeds, shoes, and sweaters were expected to be slightly scuffed and rumpled. A soft patina of age was desirable, and the total effect was a nonchalant, old-money look.

Those dozen or so basic garments listed above were not the be-all and end-all, of course. There were myriad other attractions at the Ivy shop for the dandies on campus. Paisley ties and pocket squares dyed in real "ancient madder" faded hues, whipcord olive or tan cavalry twill trousers, broadcloth tab-or club-collar shirts, cordovan or Scotch grain wingtip brogues with substantial soles, white duck cloth trousers or madras shirts for summer, and lofty lambswool turtlenecks for winter. The sophisticated young man may have splurged on a camel hair polo coat. Accessories included colorful wool surcingle belts with leather ends and brass horseshoe-shaped buckles, colorful Argyle socks, tartan cashmere scarves, silk paisley pocket squares, Tattersall waistcoats, brightly striped ribbon watch bands, and tweed flat caps.

This, however, was where the options ended. For most students at the time, the subtleties of double-breasted blazers and grenadine neckwear, suede shoes, safari jackets, enameled cuff links, covert cloth chesterfields, and Irish linen odd trousers weren't even imaginable. But then neither were exterior logos, microfibers, or designer jeans. There was also never the question of *what* to wear *when*. We all seemed to know when the occasion called for a jacket and tie, and gym clothes were confined to the gym. It was, as they say, a simpler time.

I purchased my first Ivy League gear when I was a high school freshman—a gorgeously muted grey-brown herringbone Harris Tweed sports jacket, blue button down, and penny loafers—from our local department store in Allentown,

Pennsylvania, which had an Ivy League corner within the traditional men's area (later these areas would be called "boutiques"), as did most good department stores around the
country. Often these areas would be wood-paneled and have a
leather wingback and tartan carpeting to give them the ambi-
ence of an old-fashioned university club. But the real passage,
the moment my life seemed to change in one of those rarely
obvious ways, was when I walked into a proper campus shop
for the first time.

This was in Bethlehem, Pennsylvania, in 1956, and the shop
was called the Tom Bass Shop. It was the campus shop that
served several area higher academic institutions in Pennsylvania's Lehigh Valley: Moravian, Muhlenberg, and Lafayette Colleges and Lehigh University. I was a junior in high school, but I
thought I'd joined the Big League. And in a sense, I had; just a
few years later, Tom Bass would be written up as one of the finest campus shops in the country by *GQ*.

The Tom Bass Shop was stocked to the ceiling in Scottish
sweaters and English raincoats, heathery Harris Tweed jackets in
fall and grey-and-white-striped seersuckers in spring. The piles of
solid and striped oxford cloth button-downs were pastel heaven,
and a brass wall rack of cascading rep-striped silk neckwear took
a young man's breath away.

The options still boggle my mind all these years later. There
was, as I've mentioned, a trend for madras: not just sports jackets
and trousers, but also shorts, bow ties, hat bands, swim trunks,
sports shirts, even watch wristbands done in the colorful "bleeding" cotton cloth from India, a fabric that only looked better as it
was washed and the colors ran into each other. Both khakis and
flannel trousers were styled with cinch belts just above the rear
pockets, the famous "belt-in-the-back" sign of authenticity. Real
ancient madder ties were also a sure sign of the true and trusted,
as were the wool challis paisleys, which perfectly accessorized
a tweed jacket. Many young men and women really did put a
penny in their Weejun (after "Norwegian," for the country on

whose footwear they were modeled) penny loafers. You could tell a genuine Shetland crewneck by its saddle shoulder, and anyone wearing clean white bucks was a wet smack novice, in the same way that a London Fog or Aquascutum balmacaan raincoat was never really clean.

There were dozens upon dozens of these second-tier Ivy League clothiers—second tier only because the big-name shops all had custom tailoring services and usually only private labels—providing first-quality labels such as Gant, Troy Guild, and Sero (shirts); London Fog, Burberry, and Aquascutum (raincoats); Corbin (trousers); Southwick and Norman Hilton (tailored garments); Alden and Bass (shoes); Pringle, Alan Paine, and Corgi (sweaters); duffle coats (by Gloverall); and other beloved brands of high quality now beyond memory.

As all of these labels (many of them still familiar) attest, Ivy style has had a long history—and a long prehistory, as well. My friend Christian Chensvold, who has the esteemed *Ivy Style* blog, has accurately categorized its pre- and post-1950s incarnations into distinct eras:

The Exclusive Years: 1918 to 1945. F. Scott Fitzgerald, the Jazz Age, Country Clubs, the Eastern Establishment Elite.
The Golden Age: 1945 to 1968. The Eisenhower and Kennedy Years, to Viet Nam and the Summer of Love and Woodstock.
The Dark Years: 1968 to 1980. Hippies to Preppies and Ralph Lauren.
The Great Resurgence: 1980 to the 21st Century. From Preppy and the Japanese Ivy rebels to Heritage Chic.

As Christian notes, from the gradual disappearance of Ivy League style in the mid-1960s until around 1980, Ivy style clothing was successfully manufactured and sold only by Ralph Lauren (although other designers tried). Lauren's first collection was a group of wide ties in imitation of the "kipper" tie introduced by

British designer Michael Fish. They came out the same year as Woodstock. You might have thought there couldn't have been a worse moment, but Lauren had been an alumnus of Brooks Brothers, and he had the eye and taste level to be a superb editor of the look. He took what he knew about Brooks, Chipp, and J. Press and edited his collection into an Anglo-American range of menswear that was full of bright pastels, tweeds, gray flannel, and old school ties. My own feeling is that he did more to keep Harris Tweed alive in those dark years than anyone else in the clothing business. They should erect a statue to him in the Hebrides.

Lauren is the legitimate godfather of Preppy. He held on to and expanded the genre when other American designers had given it up in favor of more European looks: the super-broad-shouldered look that Giorgio Armani propagandized in the '70s, for instance, or the Carnaby Street look, a debacle that is almost beyond description in the realm of tastelessness. But following your own lights can pay off, and Lauren became a beacon of taste in that otherwise bleak era. The tie-dyed, flower-power, grubby revolutionary look and the Italian Superman look have both disappeared, and Ivy is still here.

Ralph Lauren is still here too, joined by American Ivy interpreters such as Thom Browne and Michael Bastian, a host of smaller design labels, blog sites, and e-commerce stores, and a plethora of Japanese labels and manufacturers, each of which has adopted this uniquely American look in their own way. Brooks, owned by an Italian corporation, may have gone international, but Ivy style remains the most enduring genre of American dress, from its early-twentieth-century origins to its evolving incarnations today.

15

MAINTENANCE

MUCH OF THE DRUDGERY OF domestic cleaning is thankfully in the past. Improved hygiene, chemical solvents, colorfast dyes, synthetic fibers, and vast improvements in fabric-making machinery have all played their part to free us. They have made maintenance an almost antique word today when it comes to clothing, or anything for that matter, because we have tended to live more and more in a throwaway world. We don't maintain things these days; we replace them.

But this trend toward disposability may soon be reversed. My prediction is—and, believe me, I don't really enjoy the role of prophet—that prices of quality goods will continue to escalate (because of both the shortage of quality raw material and the increased price of quality labor), and maintenance will become even more important in the coming years for those who reject the charms of the disposable and throwaway, the cheap and shoddy. And with this in mind, I want to offer some advice on the subject. Nothing terribly technical or involving, these tips are rather a blend of common sense and experience. Tried, tested, and true, you might say.

I want to start from the philosophical point that luxury is the best bargain. That's what "the best that money can buy" means. I'm not advocating that men should buy a lot of clothes, or that they should buy the most expensive. Actually both of these approaches are wrongheaded. What I do think is that a man should buy the best he can afford and not worry about so-called bargains. The best bargain is the definition of quality. We've all gotten into the habit of considering only the initial outlay of money, and that's a costly mistake. We should really be thinking in the longer term.

Good clothes can—and will, if you maintain them—last for decades and remain good-looking, feel better and look better, while cheap garments tend to be ill-fitting and go out of style in a season or two. If they last that long. If you have good clothes, moreover, you want to keep them and wear them for many years. Simply put, you get more mileage out of better clothes. Of course, if you're the sort of person who throws everything out at season's end and buys the newest and latest fashions, any reasonable advice is a waste of breath, and you are advised to stop reading. I'm interested in a bit of reasonable *conservation* and longevity rather than short-term *consumption*.

Longevity and maintenance go hand in hand. It's often said that clothes are like friends: they become more dear with age. But clothes and friendships must both be kept in repair too. They must be attended to, treated with respect, tenderness, and loving courtesy. A small tear should be dealt with, or it may turn into an unmendable rupture.

Maintenance in clothing comes in two forms: daily and professional. We should all take care of our clothes on a daily basis, as well as knowing when to get professional help. As a daily routine, the ideal is (1) to *rotate* garments, in order to allow them to rest between wearings; (2) to clean and air them after wearing, which means brushing fabrics with a soft brush to remove dust and wiping shoes to remove dirt, and then leaving them in a space open enough for air to circulate (to evaporate perspiration)

for at least twenty-four hours; and (3) to store them properly in a closet or some other storage facility such as an armoire. On this last point, it pays to make the small investment in decent wooden hangers on which to rest tailored garments (knitted garments should never be hung; they should be folded) and in wooden shoe trees with which to maintain the shape of shoes.

Professional help is another matter. Alterations tailors, laundries, dry cleaners, and shoe repair shops are essential to proper maintenance of good clothes. Tailors, shoemakers, and shirt makers will all be happy to repair and rejuvenate their own garments, but some will balk at renovating the work of other makers. In that case you'll need specialists who can repair, alter, or clean your clothes.

While I'm on the subject of cleaning, I should also note that I'm opposed to overdoing it in this department. Because of advertising, one suspects, Americans seem to have an absolute mania for cleanliness that passeth all understanding—but generally, spots, stains, wrinkles, and a bit of dust don't do as much damage to fabrics as overprocessing does. Unless the situation is extreme, there's little reason to have tailored garments or even sweaters cleaned after every wearing. Cleaning with chemical solvents and pressing weaken (that is, break and dry out) fibers so they become shiny, flat, and lifeless. Localized treatment for spots is best, and don't mind a few wrinkles either. Good flannels, tweeds, linens, and cottons actually look better after they've been well broken in.

With all of that said, good dry cleaners, laundries, and shoe repair shops can be worth their weight in gold when you have a problem that home remedies alone won't fix. Finding these experts, however, is usually a hit-and-miss search. I wish I had an easy answer to this problem, because almost every week someone asks me for recommendations about maintenance professionals, and more often than not I'm forced to disappoint them.

What I *have* found is that, just as good craftsmanship is not initially inexpensive, neither is good maintenance cheap. You get what you pay for. And with that maxim in mind, let's turn to general principles.

1. Read the fiber content labels on your clothing. They are affixed there by law and will tell you what the fiber content of your garment is. It's just as important for both you and any professional cleaner to know this information, as it is for you to know what caused the stains in the first place. Labels will also relate cleaning information (such as "dry clean only"), which is particularly important when dealing with synthetics and blended fabrics. Manufacturer's guidelines should always be followed.

2. Brushing and airing are still the best ways to keep clothes clean and fresh. Brush your clothes after wearing to remove dust (an abrasive that wears at the fibers), using a soft-bristled brush specifically made for the purpose, and hang the garments somewhere to ventilate and naturally evaporate any odors that might cling to the fabric. Then hang them in a clean closet, giving them a bit of room—perhaps an inch between garments—to let air circulate. Please don't just throw them on a chair, where wrinkles

and odor will set. Anyone who lets his clothes fall on the floor to lie there for someone else to pick up is beneath our concern.

The only extensive exception to this principle is knitwear, which should never be hung (because that causes stretching), but rather folded and kept on a shelf or in a drawer. Luxury knits such as cashmere may be wrapped in acid-free tissue paper to prevent wrinkles and pilling.

3. Always remove stains and spots as quickly as possible. Try the least harmful method first, and test solvents on an unimportant piece of the garment (such as the inside of a cuff or seam). It's amazing how much thoroughly rinsing fabric with cold water and then gently blotting with a clean cloth can do to remove a stain, if attended to immediately.

4. As an alternative to having a garment professionally pressed, which is in fact harmful to the fibers of the fabric, try steaming with a home steam cleaner, a boiling tea kettle, or even by simply hanging the clothes in the bathroom when you're taking a shower. Many wrinkles can be easily removed in this way. In general, iron and press clothes as little as possible, since it causes wear, makes the fabric shiny, and breaks the fibers, particularly at the creases. And if you must iron, it's best to not iron directly on woolens or silks. Use a slightly damp and clean cotton or linen cloth (a handkerchief or tea towel will do nicely) between the garment and the iron, always start with low heat—you can always increase heat, but a too-hot iron will cause real and permanent damage very quickly—and bear down gently, as if you were stroking a cat.

5. There's no reason why you can't learn to sew on buttons properly. Indeed it's a skill that every man ought to know; with all the shoddy workmanship around today, buttons are bound to come flying off and usually at completely inappropriate moments—if there are any appropriate moments for buttons to fly off (rather than be undone). It seems that even good clothing today is made without concern for the proper attachment of buttons. Making these repairs yourself is quicker, cheaper, and less

harrowing than leaving it to someone else. Sewing buttons is an easy skill to be learned: use good thread (spools will say "button thread"); make sure the proper side of the button is up; use an X crossover pattern with a four-hole button, pushing the needle all the way through the layers of fabric (with practice you'll learn to do this neatly); wind some thread several times between the button and the cloth surface to form a shank; knot off and trim.

6. Alterations can be worthwhile, and an honest professional tailor can tell you which ones can reasonably be accomplished. A good tailor or seamstress can turn a shirt collar and rework cuffs—in other words, those parts of the shirt that wear out fastest—to give your shirt extra life. And don't throw away a coat because the lining is frayed; linings can be replaced. With all of that said, however, trust alterations only to competent tailors and seamstresses. A good tailor is one who works in quarter inches, and any tailor who tells you he can take in a jacket or let it out more than two inches and still have it sit properly is not a competent craftsman. A good tailor will refuse because he knows an alteration of that magnitude will completely change the line and silhouette of the garment.

Besides the obvious shortening or lengthening of sleeves and trouser legs, here are the other safe alterations:

> taking in or letting out trouser waist
> widening or tapering trouser legs
> removing cuffs
> suppressing coat waist
> easing or tightening trouser seat

The following are more difficult alterations, better left to a master tailor:

> adjusting a back or collar
> narrowing the shoulders
> narrowing lapels

lengthening or shortening a coat

easing or tightening the chest

All of these recommendations, of course, involve clothing, but what about the other rather large investment in the wardrobe, shoes? Not the hyper-engineered athletic variety of footwear made of pieced synthetic fabrics that make your feet look like they're wearing ducks designed by an anarchist. I'm talking about the leather-constructed shoe in variations of the classic designs: brogues, derbies, slip-ons, and city oxfords. Regardless of the styling, a good leather shoe is usually made entirely of fine, hardworking cowhide of one type or another, inside, outside, top, and bottom. Leathers come in a variety of weights, grains, and colors; some are even turned inside out, to produce "suede" leather. Typically fine shoes are made from fine calfskin top and inside, while the bottoms—the sole and heel—are made from toughened, more durable leathers. (For more on shoes, see Chapter 20.)

People have the most esoteric rules imaginable about polishing shoes. Favorite concoctions, secret techniques. It's enough to make you think they're talking about sex rather than footwear. Let's keep it simple.

The first point to be made about taking care of leather shoes is that they should be rotated, given a day off between each day's wearing. They should be rested in shoe trees that will stretch out the shoes and absorb perspiration; the preference is for cedar wood trees because of their absorbency and nice aroma. If the shoes are wet from rain or snow, let them dry at room temperature after removing them. Once the shoes have completely dried, wipe off any dirt with a damp cloth.

To polish the shoes, never use a liquid or silicone preparation. Only fine, high quality cream or wax polish will do. Ask a good shoe repair shop to recommend one. Cream polishes are usually applied with a cloth, wax polishes with a soft brush. Work the polish in liberally and buff, using a cloth or polishing brush. The edges of the sole and heel may be treated with the same polish, but a liquid edging solution purchased separately may also be applied without harm.

Suede shoes, which are the reverse (or hair side) of the leather, take a completely different approach. Never polish suede leathers or use synthetic sprays. The implements of choice to treat suede are the soft brush and the rubber eraser. I've found that a good brush for cleaning mushrooms is just right. Stiff wire brushes are too harsh on suede, tending to tear and remove the soft nap from the surface. When using a brush to remove dust and dirt, always brush in one direction, since the nap will follow the direction in which it's moved. If brushing doesn't remove some stains, try a rubber eraser, moving in a light circular motion over the spot.

If you're interested in shoes made from exotic skins—crocodile and alligator, lizard, ostrich, and the like—you should consult the retailer or manufacturer about maintenance. But whatever your shoe wardrobe, buy a nice shoe horn. You wouldn't want to go around with the backs of your shoes broken down any more than you would want to wear a frayed shirt collar or stained tie. As Miss Adelaide, in *Guys and Dolls*, put it, "We are a civilized people. We do not have to conduct ourselves like a slob."

16

MAXIMS

THE FRENCH NOBLEMAN François de La Rochefoucauld (1613–1680) didn't invent that most minor form of literature, the maxim. It had already been a popular party game in the salons of seventeenth-century Paris when he published his *Reflexions ou sentences et maxims morales* in 1665. But his little book did initiate the popularity of the genre. Leonard Tancock, in his introduction to the Penguin edition of the work, believes the maxim to be "the clearest and most elegant medium for conveying abstract thought known to the modern world." Whether that's precisely true or not, the form is certainly characterized by a minimum of words in the most memorable order, with an emphasis on subtlety and precision. La Rochefoucauld himself wrote few maxims about style and dress, but others have (Oscar Wilde comes immediately to mind), and indeed the maxim seems in so many ways a perfect medium for reflections on this subject.

Many of these thoughts have been pondered by others in longer, more explanatory forms. But since I can usually come up with a good opening line—it's the rest of them that give me trouble—I thought to give this genre a try.

1. *Style is the art of bending fashion to personality.*

2. *Fashion writes in bold italics, while style whispers between the lines.*

3. *It can often take an inordinate amount of thought and effort to do things simply. And a highly developed aesthetic.*

4. *A modernist aesthetic theory: the more highly developed the aesthetic sense, the more subtle and simple the style, and the more arcane the code.*

5. *Style and taste are particular sorts of intelligence.*

6. *The style of studied nonchalance is the psychological triumph of grace over order.*

7. *In matters of taste, if you can see the trees well enough, you don't have to see the forest.*

8. *There's nothing right or wrong about style. Like a poem, it simply is.*

9. *To consciously avoid fashion is itself a committed fashion.*

10. *Active sportswear makes many people look less athletic than practically anything they could otherwise wear.*

11. *In a world of plentiful and diverse choices, the hallmark of taste is restraint.*

12. *Clothes talk. In fact, they never shut up. And if you don't hear them, perhaps you aren't the intended audience.*

13. *Luxury may be, as Balzac said, less expensive than elegance. But both are less expensive than fashion.*

14. *Uniforms both include and exclude.*

15. *It's much easier to get what you want if you're dressed for it.*

16. *Being inappropriately dressed has the potential to be more embarrassing than saying something stupid.*

17. *Precision in dress is the neurotic refuge of the perpetually insecure.*

18. *It's very difficult for aesthetic judgments to transcend the culture of the judge.*

19. *The guise of nonchalance is intended to imply a strength held in reserve.*

20. *Most people think they're buying style when in fact they're only buying clothes.*

21. *Designers create fashion for anyone, but only the individual can create a style for himself.*

22. *Dressing decently should be a matter of politeness, if nothing else.*

23. *Dabblers in fashion are the most manipulated of people.*

24. *Clothes are social tools, like language, manners, and a sense of humor.*

25. *Real style is never a matter of right or wrong. It's a matter of being yourself. On purpose.*

17

MIXING PATTERNS

WEARING CLOTHES WITH FLAIR and personality is mainly a matter of pattern. Patterns, that is. The plural is what's truly important here.

All by itself, mixing patterns can be a minefield of potential disaster, but it's the perfect way to separate yourself from the madding crowd, and get the highest marks as a sophisticated boulevardier—a man of taste and quality. Let's take a few tips from the experts in the field.

If we look at consummate men of style objectively, we see several principles at work in their tailored wardrobes. Their clothes are always well fitted, and they tend to stay away from large patches of bright color. Most also are adroit at mixing patterns based on a sense of scale and proportion. They know that clashing patterns (note to self: try to sell "Clashing Patterns" as name for rock group) invariably result from disregarding scale.

If you're going to wear bold stripes, pachydermatic plaids, and bright checks together, you may well delight the children, but it's a bit harsh on adults' optic nerves. By varying the proportion in the various patterns, the eye is better allowed to focus on each

separately. Otherwise you come out looking like one of those mathematically inspired Escher tessellations.

The chest area is what should concern us most here—that is, coat, shirt, tie, and pocket square—since it's what most people's eyes are drawn to after the face. The obvious and simplest way to plan a pattern combination in this region might seem to be to concentrate on one patterned item. A bright tie, for example, with the remaining items as simple backdrop. Not a bad idea in itself, but the great danger is that everyone will notice the tie and not *you*. Highlighting one particular aspect of the wardrobe tends not to so much solve a problem as to create one: it tends to remove the wearer from his clothes. "Lovely tie," they'll say after you've left the party, but will they remember the man behind it? You've unintentionally created an obstacle, rather than surmounted one.

So we might consider a rule often advocated by those who have a basic understanding of clothes: never wear more than two patterns at a time. Again, nothing wrong with this in itself: it's easy to accomplish, and it does get a bit of play into the game. This seems a safe approach, and if that's as far as you care to go, well and fine. Perfectly reasonable to pattern two items of the four we're talking about here. A perfectly safe choice, albeit one that betrays a limited sartorial imagination.

At this point, let's leave the boys behind and venture forth with the connoisseurs of the art. The past master and still grand champion here is the Duke of Windsor (1894–1972), probably the most photographed man in the first half of the twentieth century. He was the perfect antithesis of Beau Brummel (see the Introduction for more on him). While Brummell turned to simplicity to make his mark, Windsor ran to baroque elaboration, albeit well within the pristine cut of the Savile Row tradition. His passion was for bright tweeds, as was his father's and grandfather's before him. District checks, windowpane plaids, bold stripes, and tartans were his true métier, and he loved to pair them with striped shirts, blaringly patterned ties, Argyle hosiery, and paisley pocket squares. Many of the more stolid British gentry and aristocracy of his time found all of this rather garish, and likened it to a music hall vulgarity. It was all something of repeated history, since his grandfather Edward VII had also been known for wearing bright tweeds, garish neckwear, green Tyrolean capes, and Homburg hats, and looked to many members of the upper class "more like some kind of foreign tenor" than a true Englishman (the words are Lytton Strachey's). And many upper-class Brits found Windsor (as a young man, as king, and as royal wanderer) "not quite our sort." He didn't mind; he really preferred night clubs to stuffy country house drawing rooms anyway.

But the duke knew what he was sartorially about. A true pioneer, he was smart enough to understand that the Victorian world of black broadcloth was over, and that color and pattern were coming into the lounge suit wardrobe. He knew, too, that the only way to wear a boldly patterned suit—like one in the famous Glen Urquhart plaids he adored—was to *soften* its effect with other patterns. A large patterned fabric for suiting can look unbearably bright if accompanied by solids. Think of a dark, chalk-striped worsted with a solid white shirt and dark solid tie. Elegant to be sure, but perhaps a bit too powerful for some occasions? Pairing it with smaller stripes in the shirt or tie reduces the harshness and overpowering effect.

The underlying goal here is really to prevent any one garment from hogging the spotlight. Balancing the scale of each pattern is a way of delineating each garment: if shirt and coat pattern were of the same scale, how would the eye know where one item began and the other left off? Solids often serve to set off patterns too much, making the edges too sharply defined and staccato, like a cutout silhouette. Laying pattern against pattern softens the edges, blurs them just enough, increases the harmony, and prevents us from focusing on one item, in a sort of trompe l'oeil effect. Particularly if there are color references that echo throughout the outfit, different patterns used subtly can serve us well.

The perfect example is the famous 1964 Horst photo of Windsor, taken at his mill house in France. The duke is wearing a navy-blue Shetland tweed suit with a large white windowpane overcheck, a smaller-patterned white-and-navy plaid shirt, and a mini-checked silk wedding tie, accessorized with an alligator belt and patterned pocket square. I don't know what this description might conjure up in your mind, but to see the photo is to understand sartorial elegance in its highest form. The image gives the impression of care without being too studied. Funnily enough, it also seems to call attention to the man and his individuality. As the good Dr. Cornel West, the stylish professor of divinity at Princeton University, said in a video interview, fashion is echo, but style is voice. And that's the whole point, isn't it?

18

POCKET SQUARES

IN SEVERAL RESPECTS THE pocket handkerchief is the most interesting and revealing of accessories because wearing one means making all sorts of nonfunctional choices: color, texture, and pattern must all be considered. Then there are the matters of placement and its relationship to other items being worn. Should it match, contrast, or merely accent the rest of the outfit? Finally, what about presentation, if we may steal a term from the food critics?

Problem is that one man's ideas of coordination is another's view of overplanned contrivance. Psychologically, accessories that are perfectly matched up tend to leave either a distinctly contrived, studied impression or the complete opposite: the feeling that the man was dressed by his wife or a salesman. On the former hand, we sense vanity and wasted time before the mirror; on the latter, a childlike inability to cope. Vanity, of course, comes off worse, because it's the *striving* that we see. The overly fussy concern that reveals social anxiety, a lack of self-assurance, not knowing who we are or what role we intend to play. These are psychologically deep waters, Watson, and ones any reasonable man will avoid.

The sensible rule here—as with the sensible rule for so many other things having to do with the individual in society—was set down by that great writer of manners and etiquette Baldesar Castiglione in his study *Il Cortigiano* (usually translated in English as *The Book of the Courtier*), published in Venice in 1528: "True art is what does not appear to be art, and the most important thing is to conceal it." (See Chapter 22 for a discussion of *sprezzatura*.)

The accessories should make a subtle rather than a studied statement. Proper business dress in particular should aim for approachable dignity rather than flamboyance. A discreet puff of silken color at the breast pocket is the acceptable extent of flair. And for a more formal attitude, white linen or fine cotton is foolproof.

Ah, yes, the matter of arrangement. Square-ended, multipoint, puffed, stuffed, or fluffed? When it comes to proper ways of wearing this accessory, history is not much help in the way of precedent, since it has seen virtually everything. Scented handkerchiefs were carried by Roman aristocrats and have been used

as fashion accessories by men and women from the Medieval period onward in Europe. A real vogue for lace ones began in the seventeenth century, coexistent with and perhaps occasioned by the use of snuff. Still later, Regency dandies sported embroidered cambric ones scented with eau de cologne, and among English gentlemen India silk squares became popular when Britain removed the custom duty from India silk in the 1820s. The frock coat, dating from the early 1830s, seems to have been the first style of jacket with an outside breast pocket, and within a decade men started to wear fancy handkerchiefs there as a decorative flounce. The short-lived Prince Albert was an aficionado, but then Albert was as clothes-loving a man as you'll find.

Since the early 1900s, pocket squares have been worn not only in the jacket breast pocket but in the vest and overcoat pockets as well. There was a fad in the 1910s for wearing a red silk handkerchief as a touch of ornamentation demurely protruding from the bosom of the evening waistcoat. In the 1920s the fashion was for the pocket square to harmonize with the necktie but not be exact in color or fabric. This led, in the 1930s, to a growing reaction against such studied coordination and a movement toward the more deliberate nonchalance of a white handkerchief positioned in the breast pocket as though it had been launched halfway above the welt opening. This was undoubtedly spurred on by the rise in colorful sportswear, which perhaps caught on because of the drab gloominess of the Great Depression.

This moment of national *sprezzatura* was short-lived. By the early 1940s there began a mania of coordination in the civilian sector that paralleled the broad wearing of uniforms during the period: identical colors and patterns in shirts, ties, pocket squares, hosiery, even underwear. It was the beginning of an era when tie-and-matching-handkerchief sets were viewed as marketing and packaging masterpieces. Many considered it the height of sophistication, while others understood it to be merely another fad. (Unfortunately, while they've mostly gone the way of the dodo, tie-and-pocket-square sets have stubbornly persisted into the present day, albeit in a limited way. It's traditionally the sort of item given as a gift by someone who is clueless to someone who is clueless. Rather like giving a bottle of wine called "Grapes of Wrath.")

The 1950s ushered in both the hegemony of American culture and the violently neat look of corporate consumerism. The "TV-fold" pocket square, so called because it was first seen in epidemic proportions on television personalities, seemed to fit the clean-cut, homogenized, understated bill perfectly. It played neatly into the regimented image projected by the Eisenhower years, when the House Un-American Activities Committee was ever watchful for deviation. The idea was to display an exact half inch of white linen straight across the entire top of the pocket welt. It was as neat and clean a symbol as short-cropped hair, shaven lawns, and Eames aluminum-framed stacking chairs. Minimalist hyper-neatness had triumphed, even though most men merely appeared as though they'd forgotten to mail a letter.

In the '60s the silk paisley square returned via London (see discussion of the peacock revolution in Chapter 9), and American men began to embrace a more European flair—up to and including their pocket squares. Fashion magazines of the time ran short courses in the arrangement of what was called "the Puff": an irregular and casual but nonetheless calculated rumple of silk bubbling discreetly from the chest pocket. The decidedly hip, like Frank Sinatra, even wore their brightly colored silk squares with a dinner jacket.

This was a big step away from isolationist fashion and toward a more transatlantic look—a significant development at a time when the ties that bound NATO were considered in need of constant repair. Sean Connery's debonair 007 sported the TV fold, but subsequent versions quickly adapted to the times.

These were the years, parenthetically, that gave us the silk eyeglass case, one end of which was designed to look like the puff handkerchief and which nicely managed to solve the delicate problem of what to do when both handkerchief and eyeglasses must go in the chest pocket. Alternately, some tailors used the technique of lining breast pockets with colorful silk, which could simply be pulled up from the pocket, a sort of built-in show square. Were we becoming as enamored of devices and contrivances as the Bond films?

Interestingly, Daniel Craig's rendition of 007—which debuted in the 2006 film *Casino Royale*—has returned to the white TV-fold handkerchief, with his razor-cut dark suits and sparkling white shirts. Is this evidence that Bond really *is* as meticulous and precise as he is cold-blooded, more licensed killer than spy master? Or that we've merely returned to a refined sense of elegance? Is the white starched pocket square simply the perfect accent to a navy double-breasted town suit, the proper echo for the crisp white or striped dress shirt and Macclesfield woven silk tie? Or does this remembrance of things past hold a comforting sentimental formality for us in these uncertain, unstable times?

But all of this musing ignores the prime reality, which is that a gentleman *should* wear a pocket square. Personal anecdote: I was fortunate enough when I was younger to have worked as stylist with the renowned fashion and society photographer Slim Aarons on several fashion shoots. He was very much the professional, a stickler for detail. He took me under his wing and explained many

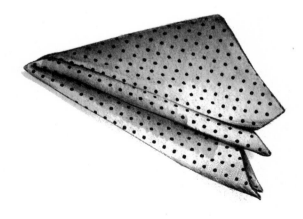

of the finer points of styling for photography. One of his sternest bits of advice was to "always make sure the man has a handkerchief in his chest pocket. It's funny, but if it's not there, when people look at the photo, they'll tell you there's something missing even if they can't put their finger on what it is."

19

SHIRTS

IT WOULD BE A GREAT DISSERVICE to begin a discussion of the shirt without quoting the wonderful poem of the same name by American poet Jane Kenyon:

> The shirt touches his neck
> and smooths over his back.
> It slides down his sides.
> It even goes down below his belt—
> down into his pants.
> *Lucky shirt.*

Lucky man.

Kenyon's poem makes the sometimes overlooked point that the shirt today—divided as it is into "business" and "sports" categories—is usually seen to exist solely in its functional appropriateness. Until the twentieth century, however, it was the garment worn most often closest to the upper body and thus had a tactile and symbolic association with the skin, as the poet so sensually discerns.

Shirts are more than a body covering or even a status symbol. We are not talking merely of cloth and thread and buttons, pricey labels, or trendy designers. We are talking about history and art, craftsmanship and tradition. Sartorial reputations have been made by a distinctive shirt collar and tie. One need only to think of the influential George "Beau" Brummell or the two dressiest of British kings, George IV and the uncrowned Edward VIII.

Historically of course it's the coat that has made the shirt what it is today. The coat as outer shell—whether doublet, frock coat, suit coat, sports jacket, or some more casual form of outer covering such as a cardigan—has compelled the shirt to put its emphasis on collar and cuffs, the visible part of the garment.

Fancy collars and cuffs came into prominence early in the Renaissance in Italy and in the English court in the sixteenth century. There's a wonderfully realistic portrait from that period in London's National Portrait Gallery of courtier Sir Henry Lee (painted 1568 by Antonio Mor) in contrived dishabille, wearing a black jerkin over a white embroidered linen shirt with a high ruffed collar and matching shirt cuffs. It's the sort of thing that today Lacroix or Lagerfeld would riff on very nicely for their women's collections, but fancy collars and cuffs continued in masculine fashion for the next two centuries, in fact until the Regency period, when a simpler style began to evolve along with a more standard coat body and sleeve.

Since then, men's clothing has developed a tellingly arcane code of subtleties about buttons and lapel shape, collar cut and cuff size. If you don't hear these subtle voices, they're simply not speaking to you. Aesthetic judgment, as Susan Sontag noted perceptively, is really cultural evaluation. In the modern world substantial fortunes have accrued from this sort of thing, as Signor Armani and Ralph Lauren will be the first to tell you.

By the second half of the nineteenth century, simple, unadorned collars and cuffs had become the norm. Detachable plain collars were popular by then and remained so until the Duke of Windsor and his brothers started a trend for turndown, sparely cut, attached collars when they were young men about town in the 1920s. They effected a simple, clean, comfortable approach that has remained in style to this day. It's a historically understated look of democratic dimensions, with an emphasis on basically standard proportions.

The shirt collar has always been a point of discernment in male dress because it provides the focal point for the face, functioning as an inverted triangle that both points to and frames the visage above it. George Brummell and his sartorial disciple, George IV, understood this point well (see Chapter 1, which might help to explain why they were such hugely important fashion figures of the early nineteenth century). And there was a third important George who also knew the value of the shirt collar and who may have had more influence over it than any other man: Lord Byron.

It is no understatement to say that Byron invented the modern shirt collar—or at least helped to popularize the wearing of it open and with its points laid flat against the collarbone, rather than standing upright around the neck. He preferred to leave his neck free of swathing and altogether preferred the large, free-flowing collars that came to be closely associated with the Romantic poets of the era. He was considered the handsomest man of his generation—as well as one of the most degenerate—and there are numerous portraits of him in black cloaks, capes, and jackets, but always with a high and softly flowing pristine white collar framing his creamy-complexioned skin and dark brown curls. Take a look at the magnificent 1814 portrait by Thomas Phillips to see the most influential image of the Romantic Age.

Since Byron's day, the dress collar—along with the masculine wardrobe generally—has retreated into subtle, restrained discretion. As men consciously turned their collective back on frivolity and gorgeousness during the Great Renunciation (see the Introduction) and chose a spare, sober smartness befitting the professional gravitas of a rising merchant and professional bourgeois industrial class, the shirt collar shrank substantially and lost much of its flair in the process. As Richard Sennett notes, in his provocative study *The Fall of Public Man*, "In the 1830s the male costume began to subside from the flowing and exaggerated lines of Romantic dress. By 1840 the cravat lost its flamboyance and lay close to the neck. Masculine lines became simpler in these two decades, and the color of clothing more drab."

The rules for the shirt are by now considered fairly universal. Apart from the subtleties of the make or designer, there's almost unanimous agreement on turndown dress collars. Varieties of the English spread collar are considered the most formal, after which come the traditional plain points, the small rounded "club" collar, and finally the casual button-downs. The pin and tab collars are considered more decidedly in the dandyesque minority and have really not been popular for more than half a century.

The important differences between each type of collar can be broken into three categories: (1) the actual size of the collar in terms of point length and spread, nape and throat height; (2) the amount of space the collar leaves for a tie; and (3) firmness of construction. Each category comes with rules of its own, most of which are—or should be—beyond dispute.

The aesthetic rule about collar size is perfectly simple: regardless of the latest fashion rage, the smaller (in bulk—that is, height and weight) the man, the smaller the collar; the longer the neck, the higher the collar may be. Tie space, for its part, is determined by preferred size of tie knot: the larger the knot, the more tie space necessary (meaning that ties made of bulk materials or of more intricate knotting techniques generally pair best with spread-collar shirts). The third consideration is purely a matter of taste: some men prefer soft clothing generally and don't mind a few odd wrinkles and a slouchy too-cool-to-care appearance; others like a collar that won't wilt under the most arduous strain and stress. The decision really has more to do with personality than anything else. A psychiatrist once told me that

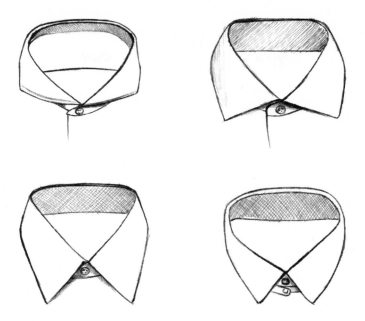

he could discover a great deal by looking at a man's collar. So could Sherlock Holmes.

Perhaps the most laid-back shirt collar is the button-down. Purposefully nonchalant, it has the appearance of dressed-down approachability. This is reflective, perhaps, of its origins as a polo shirt—literally, a shirt for polo players. The story is that, in 1900, John Brooks (retired president of Brooks Brothers and grandson of founder Henry Brooks), while vacationing in England, took in a polo match. Naturally accustomed to observing the finer points and details of dress, he was fascinated to note that the English players wore shirts on which the long collar points were buttoned down to the shirt body at their points. It was explained to him that the buttons kept the points from flapping in the face during the vigorous riding. Brooks immediately went out and bought several and shipped them home, with instructions to produce the detail and put the style in the Brooks Brothers line.

At Brooks Brothers the shirt is still referred to as a polo collar and has been so widely imitated that virtually every shirt
company does a version. Not to worry, as they say: the Brooks
button-down has never been successfully duplicated or improved
on. The classic is done in oxford cloth shirting—blue and white
are the trad colors, but yellow and pink have always been favored
by the more spirited—with precise three-and-three-eighth-inch
collar points and simple barrel cuff.

This is the kind of thing that can make a guy, as the astute
columnist George Frazier noted upon his introduction to famed
writer John O'Hara. Frazier's biographer Charles Fountain tells
the story:

> One night at Nick's, a jazz club in New York's Greenwich Village
> and a favorite hangout of O'Hara's, trumpeter Bobby Hackett, a
> friend of George's from the Boston jazz scene, brought George
> over to the author's table and introduced him. "Sit down and have
> a drink," said O'Hara warmly. "You're welcome at my table. You're
> wearing a Brooks Brothers shirt."

Since Frazier's day, of course, the button-down has experi-
enced *some* changes. For instance, some men have taken to the
idea—perhaps introduced by dandy industrial mogul Gianni Agnelli—of attaining even more dishabille by leaving the collar buttons of their button-down shirts undone.

Regardless, two timeless rules govern the button-down: (1)
there should be a good half inch of tie space between the two
points of the collar where it's attached to the collar band, but
(2) never double cuffs. The Italian interpretation of the design
has a wider point spread than its American cousin, although
both versions were as popular in the States in the '30s and
'40s as they are today. Many men will tell you a button-down
shouldn't be worn with a double-breasted suit, but Fred Astaire
and other polished film stars of the '30s and '40s did it with
panache.

The rounded club collar is the next least formal by tradition, after the button-down collar. Commonly used for boys' school uniforms, the club has always had a youthful edge. Maybe that's why it's also often favored by dandies. Think Tom Wolfe in a custom-made, chin-scrapping starched rounded collar, polka dot tie, and cream-colored suit with fedora to match.

The point collar falls in the middle of the spectrum in every way. With points of virtually any length (for example, long points, à la stylish Old Hollywood—sometimes called a Barrymore collar after the famous actor who popularized the style in the first half of the twentieth century—seem to come and go regularly), and correct with either barrel or double cuff, the point collar is the safest of business shirts. It can be worn with collar jewelry:

either a pin that actually pierces the collar or a bar that merely clips onto it. The tab collar is in fact a point collar with a built-in collar bar: tabs sewn into the collar points that button together under the tie knot. Safe, correct, appropriate, and seemly. By the way, never buy a tab collar with metal snaps: laundries tend to crush these, and then the collar is ruined.

A point collar becomes a spread collar when the angle of the points spreads more than midway between the sternum and collarbone. Often called an "English" collar because the world was introduced to the shape by the Duke of Windsor (he liked large tie knots, and this style has more space for such eccentricities), the spread collar is *the* formal business collar. There are actually two distinct spread collars: the moderate spread and the "cutaway" spread, in which the points are horizontally parallel across the neck. The cutaway speaks to a laser-like crispness and rigorous precision of almost ceremonial mood and occasion. The only more formal shirt collar is the stand-up wing style worn with evening dress (see Chapter 9).

Cuffs on these shirts can be either single (sometimes called "barrel") or double (sometimes called "French"). Either may be cut in a variety of styles, and a single cuff may take any number of buttons, although three is usually considered a prudent limit. Double cuffs take cuff links, which can mean anything from the most discreet monogrammed gold ovals to Ferrari hubcaps, although here again it's probably best to keep in mind the Sontag dictum that aesthetic judgments are cultural evaluation. The length of the shirt sleeve should be measured so that the lower edge of the cuff falls just below the wrist bone. If the coat sleeves are cut to fall just above the wrist bone, as they should be, there will be about one half inch of shirt sleeve showing. Just the right amount.

Other than that, a man has the choice of a sleeve button for the added strip of cloth (called a "placket") along the open slit between the wrist and the elbow of the shirt sleeve, a plain front or front placket (a strip of cloth running down the outside edge of the front of the shirt, where the buttonholes are), body shaping, back yoke (an additional layer of cloth across the upper back of the shirt, which may or may have pleats at its lower edge), and perhaps a chest pocket (with or without button and flap). All are optional, but some are more important than others. A pocket, for example, either with a flap or not, is purely a personal choice. Most men who wear braces (suspenders) don't like chest pockets, which makes perfect sense. And if the shirt fits well, a back yoke and pleats are really unnecessary. On the other hand, a sleeve placket button seems like a good idea to many as a way of keeping the sleeve completely closed, and laundries rather prefer front plackets. Other niceties are really just artisanal tidbits thrown in by the shirt maker.

Apart from a shirt's details and styling, there's the matter of fabric. Shirting fabrics can be almost anything woven from natural or synthetic yarn, but tradition and history have made a strong case for the Big Three: cotton, linen, and silk. Linen may well have been the first woven fabric for clothing worn next to the skin, with silk and cotton not far behind. Until the nineteenth century, a man talked about putting on "fresh linen," meaning a clean shirt. But with the rise of the great cotton mills in the north of England—all of which were supplied with the raw product by their colonies in North America and India—and a growing awareness of cleanliness, cotton became king for intimate apparel. Long staple and strong fibers that were easily dyed and washed were seen as ideal for shirts and undergarments.

Cottons are thought to be classified by their place of origin—Egyptian, pima (from Pima, Arizona, United States), Sea Island (the sea islands off the coast of Georgia, United States), and so forth—but these distinctions have been notoriously hard to maintain. I've not followed the history of the court cases having to do with the trademarking of these terms as judiciously as I should, but there has been an incredible amount of legal bother about all of them. Better to think in terms of the quality of the fiber and weave of the fabric.

For the purposes of shirting, the best cottons are long-fibered, with great strength and fineness, and a low luster and uniformity of white or pale cream color. In other words, fabric that will be smooth and crisp to the feel, that will have a luster that allows for saturated color, and that will hold up well to repeated laundering. Sea Island, Egyptian, and pima cottons all fall into this category and are the most expensive. Less expensive cottons are usually denoted not by place but by weave.

Broadcloth is the oldest and simplest weave for cotton fabric, with a plain one-to-one, over-and-under pattern using threads of the same color. Broadcloth and poplin shirting both have a slightly unbalanced weave in that the weft (or filling) yarn is a bit heavier than the warp thread. With poplin, this difference is accentuated to produce more of a ribbed effect. This is the basic shirting fabric because it's smooth, launders well, and can be produced in any pattern.

Another popular cotton cloth is chambray, which derives its name from the northern French town of Cambrai and is produced basically with the same weave as broadcloth. With chambray, however, the warp threads are colored, while the weft threads are white. Chambrays are usually plain, solid colors, but can be produced in patterns as well. Lightweight versions are used for warm-weather shirts.

Oxford cloth is also a plain weave but visually coarser because usually twice as many warp threads are used as weft threads, producing a basket-weave effect. This cotton cloth was apocryphally first woven by a Scottish cotton mill at the end of the nineteenth century, which also produced cloths representing Yale, Cambridge, and Harvard, but these latter three were overshadowed by the popularity of the oxford cloth and are no longer produced. The New York firm of Brooks Brothers did more to promote this fabric than anyone by choosing it for their famous button-down dress shirts. "Royal oxford cloth" is a finer version of this beefy shirting. Usually the warp threads are colored, while the weft threads are white, as in chambray.

An even chunkier shirting fabric than oxford cloth is twill, whose two-to-one (or similar thread proportion), over-and-under weave produces a cotton fabric with a distinctive diagonal ribbed effect. The angled ridges gives the fabric an added textural interest to shirting, anywhere from barely visible to bold depending on the number of threads combined in the weaving process.

Much lighter than any of these cotton fabrics is voile. Usually considered a summer cotton shirting because it's both lightweight and crisply springy, voile is characterized by using very fine, twisted yarns in a tight plain weave. The result is a lustrous fabric of exceptional strength for its weight. The finest voiles seem to be almost transparently gossamer yet retain their fresh feeling in the heat.

Slightly less popular than cotton for shirting, linen nevertheless remains a common fabric choice in the garment industry. When cotton became readily available in Europe in the eighteenth century, it replaced linen as a shirting fabric to a great extent, but both Irish and Italian linens are still used in men's clothing to great advantage. Both have a highly porous, cooling weave characterized by a slightly rough texture that softens from use. Irish linens tend to be heavier and are found mainly in suitings, while Italian linens are lighter in weight and used mainly for shirting fabrics. Funnily enough, in an age of the wrinkle-free, no-iron, and the highly pressed, the beauty of linen is seen in its ability to corrugate, a mark of old school elegance. Lightweight linen is found in sports shirts, business shirts, and formal dress shirts.

Rarer, and finer, than linen and cotton is silk. Its history as a clothing fiber is long and replete with myth and legend. What is known is that silk was first produced in China at least five thousand years ago and that silk cloth first reached Europe some time during the first millennium. Silk culture (the care of silkworms, now a scientifically controlled industry, but previously a time-consuming and delicately devotional enterprise) began in Constantinople in the sixth century, and by the fifteenth century

northern Italian cities had gained a reputation for fine silk production in Europe.

Silk shirting is characterized by being strong and absorbent,
with a smooth hand and lustrous appearance. Since good-quality
silk is expensive, it's always been considered a luxury fabric.
F. Scott Fitzgerald's protagonist Jay Gatsby was fond of thick,
creamy silk shirts that he ordered by the dozen, an all-time literary standard for conspicuous consumption. Today silk is only
infrequently used in business shirts, ones that are custom-made.
Otherwise silk is relegated to the sports shirt category (such as
silk batiks, seersuckers, and other styles of resort wear) and, to a
much lesser extent, used for formal evening shirts.

Cotton, linen, or silk—the fabric you choose for your shirt is
but one element in that all-important nexus where collar, tie, and
pocket square meet: the chest-to-neck area just below your face,
where so much attention is focused. No less than Alan Flusser,
that astute observer, chronicler, and wearer of finely tailored
clothes, has observed that the "triangular sector formed below
the chin by the V opening of a buttoned suit jacket constitutes
the cynosure of a man's tailored costume."

Truly, the collar-tie-pocket-square nexus is one of the two
principal areas in which a man can go badly astray in his wardrobe—one of two dangerous reefs on which a man's ship of style
can be scuttled. (The foot area, which includes the shoe, hosiery,
and trouser, is the other; see Chapter 20.) Given how fraught
with peril this nexus is, it's worth spending some time on it. I'm
not talking about how to tie a tie or fold a pocket square, mind
you; we don't need all those little educational, step-by-step line
drawings, not among friends. I suspect that if you really don't
know how to tie a tie, this book won't be of much interest to
you anyway. Rather, I want to spend some time on the area as a
whole, since it's such a crucial aspect of male attire.

Until the mid-twentieth century the question of scrutiniz-
ing and regulating this area hardly arose, because there was a
standard answer to weekday dress for most business men: white

shirt, discreet tie, and white cotton handkerchief (see Chapter 18 for a full discussion of the pocket square). It was a clean, bland, neutral look that was prized in the 1950s by many.

Since then, options have proliferated. Not only are shirt patterns and colors more interesting, and more acceptable for the office and boardroom, but there's much more choice in neckwear and pocket squares as well. Fabrics for both ties and squares include a variety of silks, wools, cashmere, linen, synthetics, and blends thereof. Some of these are worn seasonally: linens and silk shantungs seem more appropriate for summer, wool tweeds and cashmeres for winter. Today, that observation constitutes the only rule worth mentioning about fabrics for ties and pocket squares.

Undoubtedly because of the countless options at their disposal, many stylish men have noted that the collar-tie-pocket-square nexus can be tricky. The great pitfall is to have too much going on. Like the man who seems to be awash in heavy-scented cologne, rather than using just a few dabs of something light, too many patterns and colors seem to drown the appearance. It used to be argued that the solution to this problem was to use no more than two patterns out of a possible four: shirt, tie, pocket square, and jacket. This isn't nonsensical, and it's an easy rule to follow. It's just a tad dull. The use of pattern is really more an exercise in scale and balance. In short, of alternating proportions. If every pattern—in the shirt, tie, square, and jacket—is of the same scale, points of definition in the garments themselves are obliterated; barriers are erased, everything bleeds together, and the niceties of styling and cut are undermined. (See Chapter 17 for a fuller discussion of mixing patterns.)

The better solution to the problem of overpatterning is to pay attention to the varying scale of patterns. Patterns work better when they can be individually absorbed by the eye, and when the various items in the outfit can be comfortably delineated; otherwise we tend to feel as though we're sitting in an optometrist's examination room. Or at the circus.

So if the jacket is a bold check, such as a windowpane or large glen plaid, the tie might be a smaller pattern, the shirt an even smaller one, and the pocket square somewhere in between. This is only one of many ways to balance these patterns, you understand, and the greater variety can be calculated by the mathematicians among us.

The role that color plays in these matters is subtle. For instance, exactly matching tie and pocket square colors can have the unfortunate effect of making you look like a car rental agent; the point is that the tie and pocket square should *echo* each other in terms of color, rather than coordinate. There really aren't any rules about this that a novice can easily grab onto. The safest approach would be to simply keep the outfit of shirt, tie, pocket square, and jacket to a few variations of the same color. The problem is, in doing so, we tend to look a bit boring. So the idea of "reflected" color, that is, using the tie and handkerchief to reflect a subtle color in the jacket or shirt, makes a good deal of sense. In other words, high contrast should be avoided, and colors should blend rather than pop. A bright green tie or pocket square might echo the olive tone of a tweed jacket but might be so overpoweringly vibrant as to call attention to itself. And then, as I never tire of asking, when you leave the party, everyone will remember your tie, but will they remember you?

Textures of fabrics seem less important than color, except for one basic rule of thumb: respect seasonal considerations. Woolen and cashmere ties (whether woven or knitted) work well in winter not only because they're warmer, but because their thicker texture has an affinity with heavier suiting fabrics such as flannels and tweeds. Cotton, linen, and slubby silks such as shantung make more sense with summer tailored fabrics: they're lighter, airier, and more in tune with less substantial cloths used in jackets, trousers, and shirts. Fabrics are friends; they're known by the company they keep.

Apart from this, think of texture as a parallel dimension to pattern, and follow the rules outlined above. There's no need, for example, for a shantung tie to be complemented by a shantung pocket square. That would be overly fastidious and Victorian. The overriding message sent out by people who are overly fastidious, and who look as though they took most of the morning to match everything up properly, is one of blatant vanity. We know that all of us, with the possible exception of saints, are a bit vain, but there's no need to make our vanity *the* message of our lives. Suppression is not always a bad thing, in this nexus or any other.

20

THE SHOE-HOSIERY-TROUSER
NEXUS

WE ALL GO THROUGH PERIODS when we want to simplify. The first time this happened to me I got rid of all the shirt jewelry (cuff links, collar pins, tie bars) and silk pocket squares, and decided on a wardrobe of navy blazers and grey suits, tweed jackets, corduroy trousers, only blue and white shirts, and brown suede shoes with everything. A navy-blue knit silk tie would see me through. It seemed to me that I could almost get dressed with my eyes closed and still make a presentable appearance.

My thought at the time was to free myself from the concerns of coordination—and in truth, I was happy for a while. But then I gradually started adding back items. First it was the silk squares, then a few striped ties and the tie bar, and then . . . Well, you can see where this is going. It all came back and then some.

I suppose the only thing I haven't changed my mind about is the brown suede shoes. I still don't have a pair of black shoes in my wardrobe except for the black velvet Albert slippers I wear with a dinner jacket. And since I've never worn black suits, the brown suedes seem to suffice.

It's one approach, isn't it? And I don't particularly recommend it either, just because I'm a brown-shoes-with-everything guy. But I have noticed that the Northern Italians have backed me up on this: they seem to wear nothing but brown shoes, and the combination of brown shoes with a dark blue suit is an incredibly natty look whose roots are in the 1930s English style of wearing navy chalk-striped double-breasted suits with brown suede shoes à la the then Prince of Wales.

The Northern Italians are onto something else, too: that the intersection of the shoe and trouser, and the hosiery that lies between them, is one of immense importance for male appearance. Perhaps the only more important juncture than the shoe-hosiery-trouser nexus, indeed, is the collar-tie-pocket-square nexus (see Chapter 19). Yet while almost any lay observer will take in this upper nexus almost by instinct, at the same time they review their counterpart's face, the sartorially inclined beholder will reliably do a double-take—looking down quickly to the second nexus, the one where the man meets the pavement, or the parquet. Indeed, it is precisely because it is so often overlooked that the shoe-hosiery-trouser nexus is of such monumental importance, for it reveals exactly how far the style of the subject extends.

Let's start with the shoe, as I just did. And here let's assume we're talking about proper shoes made of real leather, unscuffed and polished. Not shoes worn in the gym or on the track. The question is, How much of the leg line do you wish the shoe to be?

Some people are of the opinion that the foot should be considered part of the leg, and the shoe should be as close as possible to the color of the trousers in order to maintain a sight line without a break. This school of thought also holds that the hosiery should blend seamlessly into the monochromatic field. For those who consider the foot to be an extension of the leg, black shoes are a necessity with navy, charcoal grey, or black suits in order to maintain a minimum of disruption. This approach would also recommend dark hosiery of approximately the same color and shade as the suit. Continuity and uniformity govern here, and not a bad thing either. It makes for neat dressing, foolproof—unless you're color-blind—and entirely proper. The drawback is not that it's devoid of personality; it's merely boring for both the wearer and the viewers.

Obviously some still firmly believe the path to respectability is trod with black shoes. But then respectability isn't what it used to be, and neither are aesthetics. Nothing looks smarter than a pair of top-quality, perfectly polished black shoes, but that's the catch, isn't it—there's nothing more to be said?

One of the problems is that black shoes are uniformly black, and that most of them have a simplicity of design that only adds to their puritanical aspect. There was a period, roughly the third quarter of the twentieth century, when the Gucci black leather slip-on with the snaffle bit hardware ruled the fashion roost, but that was more of an aberration than anything else. A black shoe is a symbol and artifact of pristine simplicity. For instance, the Regency beaux set down the rules about black shoes, and their Victorian grandchildren made the rules ritual: for instance, they were the only color of shoes allowed in town, or in the evening, or on Sunday, or on other formal occasions. Black shoes were considered de rigueur for business and formal occasions; preachers preached against not wearing black shoes in church. It was one of the bulwarks against barbarianism. But then the Victorians were choked with anxiety and had dozens of rules for everything. They were mad for categorization. Best to leave them with their neuroses.

The other way to regard the shoe is as a completely separate field for design and exhibition, a true accessory rather than an extension. This is not as uncontroversial as it may sound; as late as 2002, fashion footballer David Beckham—that very year voted one of Britain's best-dressed men—was criticized in the press for wearing brown shoes with a blue suit. Yet for most of us, the rules about brown shoes—my favorite, and the closest thing to black shoes on the spectrum of formality—have gone the way of spats and top hats. Today brown shoes in the evening no longer betray a person's lack of social breeding. Actually, I can't think of anything that does, but never mind.

There was a time, to be sure, when brown shoes of any sort were something of a mark against a man. May I introduce you— or perhaps reacquaint you, if you've read the great American novel *Sister Carrie* (published 1900), by Theodore Dreiser—to one of the charming rogues of literature, Mr. Charles H. Drouet, traveling salesman. The time is August 1889, on a train to Chi-cago: "His suit was of a striped and crossed pattern of brown wool, new at that time, but since become familiar as a business suit. The low crotch of the vest revealed a stiff shirt bosom of white and pink stripes. . . . The whole suit was rather tight fit-ting, and finished off with heavy-soled tan shoes, highly polished, and the grey fedora hat." It should already be clear that Charley Drouet is something of a rascal. Dreiser meant his characters' clothes to speak for them, and it's telling that Drouet wore not just brown shoes but tan ones, and with a heavy sole that added to the literal rudeness of his outfit. What nuance his brown shoes contain! Black is always black, but that brown is sometimes tan is a notion worth remembering.

Brown shoes run the gamut of shades from creamy bisque to darkest mahogany in either polished leather or suede. This of course in itself opens a pit of problems. The question is, Which shade best suits your mood and attire? Taupe? Tobacco? Chest-nut? Espresso? The old rule was that the shoe should be just a shade darker than the trouser, and this continues to make sense, apart from tropical dress, in which white shoes have an aristo-cratic heritage of ubiquity. Brown shoes do tend to break the sight lines, but that can be a good thing, both because it provides more variety and also because it gives the eye another point of focus.

Brown shoes also open the door to brighter hosiery, which brings us to the third element of this nexus. Whereas socks once used to be demure—all blacks and blues and greys—today a bit of flair is accepted, even expected. Argyles have a long history in sportswear, but why not wear them with a city suit as long as there's some tonal connection? Or striped socks, à la Fred Astaire in *Flying Down to Rio*. Or a humorous motif like pink flamingos, skull & crossbones, unicorns, or just some colorful spots?

Today we're more ruled by mood than propriety. This makes things a bit more difficult, on the one hand, because we no longer have the guidance of the rules, but on the other hand many of the rules of dress have been seen to be rather arbitrary, silly, and stifling. The novelty of wearing what a person wants can be refreshing—wearing what one wants, that is, within reason.

Which brings to mind the matter of socklessness. Many men in the period between World Wars I and II discovered the joys of tropical climes (see Paul Fussell's wonderful account of travel during this period, *Abroad*), which also meant the discovery of such items as walking shorts, espadrilles and moccasins, berets, striped jerseys, and silk suits. Going sockless became a poignant image of sunshine, health, and leisure.

The idea was next taken up on Ivy League campuses in the United States, a hothouse of casual dress. Very casual footwear such as the famous L. L. Bean camp moccasin, the slip-on Weejun, and tennis shoes were campus staples that didn't need socks. Not that dorm life lent itself to scrupulous laundering habits anyway.

Of course men have been wearing their Albert slippers around the house without socks forever—but, as one of the markers of true sangfroid, the sockless look is now seen on men wearing suits and wing-tip brogues. This is both extreme and wrong for two reasons. First, there are compelling, health-related reasons for having next to the skin absorbent garments that can be changed and laundered frequently; that's the whole point of underwear, isn't it? Second, this blatant attempt at nonchalance seems rather amateurish and weak as a ploy, a much too studied and obvious way of showing insouciance. Not to mention that once you reach such a level of deafening obviousness, you've turned whatever idea you're toying with into a cliché.

I'm a forgiving person myself, but a man who wears a business suit and town shoes without socks as some sort of fashion statement—rather than simply being a major loon—is probably capable of sitting on the wrong end of a shooting stick. It's fine for men in the fashion business to do this sort of thing; they can't help themselves. But, dear reader, this look is not right for you.

21

SHORTS

O F COURSE WE HAVE THE GOOD PEOPLE of Bermuda
to thank. Not for actually inventing shorts, but for enlarging
our vision of the garment's potential, putting it into a completely
different category—upscaling it, if you will. Until the male Bermudian showed other men by stunning example that we could
wear shorts in a more formal way, we'd always thought they—
the shorts, not the Bermudians—were either military, athletic, or
generally just very casual resort items.

The early 1950s Bermuda Experiment—and that's just the
name I'm giving it—convinced us that shorts actually had a
much wider sartorial range than we had supposed, and we began seeing them in a completely new light. The experiment's
importance was only slightly mitigated in practice by never really having caught on much outside the British territorial island,
but never mind that. It's still an incredibly interesting stylistic
and utilitarian idea. Indeed I don't think it's a stretch to say that
shorts might have been the first casual business wear.

For some reason men resist showing a bit of leg, even in soar-
ing heat and humidity. We're rather stubborn, I'm afraid, and
not a little overly concerned for our dignity. We seem to need

165

an excuse—being on a basketball court, soldiering in the desert, being close to a beach—to shed twenty completely unnecessary inches or more of flapping trouser leg. You may want to argue with me about this, but I suspect there's still a bit of Victorian propriety clinging to this issue. I don't have a horse in the race, since I'm a bit long in the tooth to expose a lot of skin, but why shouldn't younger men working in warmer climes (whether seasonal or not) be both fashionably *and* sensibly as comfortable as they can under the circumstances? I merely ask.

Historically, shorts are related to sports and military uniforms, as so much of men's clothing is. According to W. Y. Carman's *A Dictionary of Military Uniform*, shortened trousers were worn by native soldiers in the British army in South Ghana as early as 1873. It's known that khaki shorts were worn by some British soldiers in India by the turn of the twentieth century, and they undoubtedly wore them as mufti (civilian dress) when they returned to Britain. These shorts were in fact copied from the dress of the famous native fighters in the Brigade of Ghurkas, the unit of the British Indian Army comprised of Nepalese soldiers who had fought with the British in India since the early nineteenth century. These fierce warriors were known for their deadly kukris (long, curved knives) and their wide, short trousers. You can see this garment quite clearly on a memorial statue at the Ministry of Defense in London of one such Ghurka soldier in the traditional uniform. The shorts are characterized by their wide leg and self-belted waist; sometimes the hem was even cuffed. Comfortable and durable, they continue to find admirers and are a solid summer component of the military chic look some men seem to enjoy even all these years later.

It makes sense that, from the military, shorts would make their way into a man's wardrobe through warm weather sports. As authors Robert Graves and Alan Hodge point out, the most popular sport of '30s Britain was hiking. Leisure, amateur sports came into their own after World War I. Hiking clubs were sponsored by local newspapers particularly popular in Europe in the

1920s, since hiking was both a cheap holiday and considered generally healthful. Railways offered inexpensive fares to the countryside. The standard walking uniform for tramping about the Alps, Black Forest, Shropshire dales, French chateau region, or Piedmont was a stout knitted sweater, khaki shorts, heavy socks, sturdy country boots or shoes, and rucksacks. "Ramblers," as hikers were called, seemed to be everywhere there was a mole-hill or meadow.

It wasn't long before other athletic types began catching the bug. First shorts turned up on golf courses. When it comes to dress, golfers always have had less inhibitions than the rest of us, and shorts on the green were just the next step after the plus fours—baggy trousers cut off four inches below the knee and fastened just below the knee with a strap-and-buckle, a close cousin of knickerbockers—already seen on every course in the world in the 1920s. Then, before you could say "knobby knees," shorts were on the tennis court. In 1932 Bunny Austin, Britain's top-ranked player, caused something of a sensation at the men's US National Championships in Forest Hills, Long Island, when he appeared courtside wearing white flannel shorts instead of the de rigueur white flannel trousers. Shorts had actually been worn for some time on tennis courts, but Austin gave the fashion his impeccable imprimatur, and the less restrictive, cooler garment probably helped his game. (A study of the effects of costume on sports records has, sadly, yet to be done, but it does appear that the breaking of sports records runs in tandem with the march toward lighter-weight and less cumbersome sports uniforms. It would seem to stand to reason that if a tennis player, for example, weren't encumbered in heavy layers of restricting cloth—as both men and women were in the nineteenth century—he might play a more lively game. And of course, tennis [not to mention other sports] has indeed gone from a rather airy gentlemanly pastime to a vigorous, intense workout.)

By the 1950s, "walk shorts" had entered the wardrobe of every American collegiate young man, to the point that some

manufacturers began producing three-piece suits of coat, trousers, and walk shorts specifically for this market. After World War II, men "seemed anxious to make up for the years of conformity that war had imposed. A direct result of this new assertiveness was the sudden surge in the popularity of walk shorts, which in 1949 were being seen on campuses and at smart resorts."

Although the military influence of wearing khaki shorts clung to men's fashions even after the conclusion of the war, the American man eventually began to wear walk shorts "in everything from solid colors to eye-catching plaids, dominant checks, and bold stripes." In any event, by the time walk shorts swept the United States, there could be no doubt that shorts had now gained acceptance across the board, or that they could and would be worn on dressy-casual occasions of every sort, including country club dances, boating parties, and other events of the weekend calendar. Fabrics and colors had come a long way since the khaki days of the '20s; now it was all bold and pastel hues and patterns of bleeding madras plaids, awning striped poplins, cotton tartans, candy-striped seersucker, and bright polished cotton twills.

Yet as so often happens, unwritten but rigid rules regarding this new staple of the man's wardrobe quickly evolved. They all revolved around hosiery. At the most casual end of the style spectrum, shorts could be worn with almost any shirt (oxford button-down, polo, boatneck pullover) and any sort of slip-on footwear (deck shoe, moccasin, penny loafer) with short socks or no socks. But as soon as dark, over-the-calf hosiery entered the picture, the outfit became immediately more formal. Dressier hose required a dressier shirt, even a tie and sports jacket. It was rumored that there were men who had tuxedo suits with evening shorts, accompanied by traditional black silk hose and patent pumps.

Shorts and their accompaniments have gone through something of a downgrading since then. The ubiquitous uniform in much of America, for instance, now seems to be composed of cargo shorts, T-shirt, and hyper-designed running shoes. It's a decent enough look, I suppose, if your only goal is comfort. And all those expandable pockets do come in handy for all the stuff—water bottle, latest iPad or iPhone, keys, wallet, antidepressant medication—so many of us seem to cart around with us these days.

Perhaps I shouldn't quibble. While shorts have undergone a sort of degrading in some corners, in others they retain their Bermudian zest. For example, the neo-preppy look has spurred a renewed interest in patchwork madras, seersucker, colorful cotton twills, and linens, all of which work quite well with shorts. Why not indeed wear a pastel chambray shirt, natty foulard bow tie, and lightweight blazer with a pair of patchwork madras shorts? Or a softly creased, tobacco-hued linen pair with a cream-colored safari jacket, a bright bandana tied at the neck? With a pair of either burnished bench-made slip-ons or espadrilles of course. Now you're talking summer!

22

SPREZZATURA

"**D**O NOT INQUIRE TOO DEEPLY** into the truth of other people's appearance," the renowned advisor and letter writer Lord Chesterfield cautioned his son. "Life is more sociable if one takes people as they are and not as they probably are."

I know I've mentioned this quote before, but how refreshing! How delightful! A little well-intentioned hypocrisy. It's an important lesson we seem to have forgotten, this idea that civility rests on the little lie, the sin of omission, the harmless compliment, the overlooked slight, the tiny fabrication, the artful ability to conceal effort and inappropriate passions. These little niceties—manners, they used to be called—are the grease on the wheels of social friction.

Nowadays there seems to be a lot more friction and a lot less grease. And all the sparks that fly around as a result seem to play into our general sense of overexcitement. Somehow we've come to hold the rather naive and nasty belief that public and private life should be indivisible. Or rather that people shouldn't have private lives at all. But are we really the better for casting our nosy, titillating little flashlights into everyone's linen basket? It may well be time for a little hypocrisy, if we are to have any privacy left. Call it *defensive irony*.

Isn't it time we reacquainted ourselves with the virtues of a civil style? Or has the horse already left the barn, and our media frenzy for transparency completely usurped our right to privacy? As Jill Lepore pointed out in an article on surveillance in the *New Yorker*, "There is no longer a public self, even a rhetorical one. There are only lots of people protecting their privacy, while watching themselves, and one another, refracted, endlessly, through a prism of absurd design." Can we not return to a style of social philosophy in which decorum and propriety are maintained in public discourse, even at the expense of a bit of agreed-on hypocrisy? History is full of fine examples of civil styles that grant the frailties of people. I'm thinking, for example, of a writer such as La Rochefoucauld, whom even Voltaire credited with greatly contributing to forming the taste and style of the French nation during the age of Louis XIV. Or Lord Chesterfield, whose letters to his son illuminate the social climate of Georgian England. But the man who delineated its proprieties of civil style and explained the difference between "poise" and "pose" best was Baldesar Castiglione, the great Italian Renaissance codifier of behavior, in an age of great codifiers. His treatise, *The Book of the Courtier* (first published 1528 in Venice), was written as a handbook for gentlemen, a compendium of the ideals of public behavior at the moment of the Italian Renaissance's greatest splendor.

The book's theme is the question of how a person should represent himself to others, how he should deport himself in the public arena. Castiglione's contribution to the literature of etiquette is the idea that civility cannot really be perfect unless accompanied by a sense of gracefulness (*la grazia*) and that the perfection of this refinement is achieved and perceived through a sense of style he defines as *sprezzatura*. As he writes, "I have discovered a universal rule which seems to apply more than any other in all human actions or words: namely, to steer away from affectation at all costs, as if it were a dangerous reef, and to practice in all things a certain nonchalance [*sprezzatura*] which conceals all artistry and makes whatever one says or does seem uncontrived and effortless."

Castiglione's explanation for the importance of this "universal rule" of nonchalance is that, funnily enough, most people are willing to believe that a trivial fault can belie greatness: "A man who performs well with so much facility must possess even greater skill than he does, and that if he took greater pains and effort he would perform even better." The purposeful too-cool-to-care look has been around a long time indeed.

In English the word Castiglione uses to define his "universal rule," *sprezzatura*, is usually rendered as "nonchalance," but in truth it's more than that. *Sprezzatura* is not merely unreflective spontaneity, or casual thoughtlessness, or even the attempt to lie or deceive. It isn't, in short, recklessness. Quite the opposite: it is the conscious attempt to appear natural, the affectation that seems uncontrived, the studied casualness and feigned indifference that is intended to indicate a greater worth than one actually sees. It is the ability to conceal effort—the opposite of affectation, which exposes itself.

In more modern times the British writer Stephen Potter composed a humorous book on the subject, titled *The Theory and Practice of Gamesmanship or The Art of Winning Games Without Actually Cheating.* Potter referred to contrived nonchalance as "gamesmanship" and codified a number of gambits and ploys to fit every occasion in which a person might want to show a sense of innate superiority. In a sense, Potter actually wrote down the unwritten rules that may govern the competitive struggles of life. It's Castiglione lite—a wonderful bit of satire and a great read.

Yet *sprezzatura* is different from gamesmanship, in that it's not innately antagonistic or competitive. Rather, it is motivated by civility; it is that subtle sense of ease and charm and tradition that hides the forces at work, the disorder, the difficulties, the effort. The psychological result is the effect of careless mastery that takes the viewer in and gives him that unexpected lift we find so fulfilling.

By now you may be seeing the connection between *sprezza-tura* and sartorial style. That most elegant of Cavalier poets, Robert Herrick (1591–1674), explained the relationship nicely in his poem on derangement in dress, "Delight in Disorder":

> A sweete disorder in the dresse
> Kindles in cloathes a wantonnesse:
> A Lawne about the shoulders thrown
> Into a fine distraction:
> An erring Lace, which here and there
> Enthralls the Crimson Stomacher:
> A Cuffe neglectfull, and thereby
> Ribbands to flow confusedly:
> A winning wave (deserving Note)
> In the tempestuous petticote:
> A carelesse shooe-string, in whose tye
> I see a wilde civility:
> Doe more bewitch me, then when Art
> *Is too precise in every part.*

This sense of contrived grace, those little flurries of purposely unbuttoned haphazardness became an aesthetic ideal in various eras, and not just in dress. It can be seen in all sorts of design. The English garden of the eighteenth century for example—with its meadows, and copses, and gentle lawns and bowers—perfectly shows the attempt of art to conceal effort by making the design appear to be following nature. Contrast the English meadow style with the intricate ornateness of the formal French gardens of the period, meant to impress the viewer with the determination of man to subdue nature to his own ambition and aesthetic sense of rational opulence. Or, as I believe playwright George S. Kauffman once said, "to show what God could have done if He'd have had money."

But of course it's in fashion where the aesthetics and social aspects of *sprezzatura* most closely align. As Castiglione explains, the great virtue of *sprezzatura* is that it implies a great-ness unseen, a potential implicit in its very subtleties and flaws, a strength held in reserve. It's an approach that was valued by English Cavaliers and Regency Bucks, in Jacksonian America and Directoire France. It's the English country house look (see Chapter 8) and its American cousin, the understated Ivy League style (see Chapter 14), with its modestly unpadded sack suits, rolled button-down collars, and the sheer casualness of wearing penny loafers and Argyle socks with a suit. An artful blend of the blandly correct with the colorfully casual. It's the loose, seem-ingly underconstructed, and comfortable suits of Italian style (discussed in Chapter 13), not to mention their inimitable habit of mixing and matching clothing from various other subgenres of style (more on which below). All of these styles are as venerable pronouncements of purposefully exaggerated understatement as can be found today within the realms of modern taste.

Even the most nonchalant national styles have recently lost some of their *sprezzatura*. The neo-preppy look, an offshoot of Ivy League style, has come to reign globally, from Tokyo to Toledo, but with not quite the *sprezzatura* intact. These days there seems to be a certain feverishly engineered feeling about it, as if a great deal of anxiety has resulted in it being *obviously* carefree in a stage-managed sort of way. It has contemporarily blended with the School of Cool. Call it perhaps "postmodern preppy cool." The motives and approach are of a studied nonchalance, but the result seems rather too blatant to be completely effective, since the effort is not hidden. And as we know, *ars est celare artem* ("art is to conceal art"), as my aunt Gladys used to say.

An idea closely related to—but importantly different from—*sprezzatura*, "cool" was a term first used by African Americans to denote someone who had his emotions under control in times of stress and tribulation. Cool came to be associated with "hip," the American form of French existentialism that was associated with a disdain for the conventional and an ability to carry on with-out assurance. After World War II, it was a counterculture revolt against the bourgeois work ethic and corporate consumerism, last seen generally in the flower children of the 1970s. Symbolic clothing associations here run the gamut from James Dean to tie-dyed. In its mode and aim to hide the emotions, to present an appearance that hides effort and care, that belies intention, cool is a decidedly American approach to studied nonchalance.

But for those of us who aren't either hipsters or hippies, counterculture characters or public poseurs, how can we achieve that cultivated insouciance which acts as a defensive buffer between public and private? There are few rules—well, not even rules really, perhaps points of note: (1) A preference for the mildly rumpled over the new and shiny. The oft-attributed Nancy Mitford comment on interior design bears mentioning in this connection: "All nice rooms are a bit shabby." (2) A touch of sentimental, personal eccentricity. (3) A marked tendency toward clothes that at least appear comfy. And (4) the idea of counterpoint, based on a total sense of confidence. Noel Coward provided a useful example of what we might call "counterpoint etiquette," when he discovered he had worn evening dress to an occasion where everyone else was in daytime attire. (See Chapter 9 for the full story.)

Simply put, what's important to one person shouldn't be important to another, and vice versa. A few good wrinkles always separate the men from the boys, because invariably the novice tries to appear flawless and correct—and that's his great mistake, and the trap is easily set and sprung. The old ploy used to be to shine the light on this attempt to be immaculately proper and drive it into the ground. "How do you manage to always look so sharp? I never seem to have the time to get all matched up." And keep repeating this and similar comments over and over until everyone's aware of his vanity and shallowness.

Sprezzatura is a matter of reaching for perfection, while cultivating the impression of never having given it a thought. It's the sense of *ease*, the air of never having prepared, that wins the day. The man who's all color coordinated is the one, we feel, who blatantly tries too hard. His clothing sends a clear message: he's insecure. Contrast this man with Fred Astaire, who often wore a button-down shirt with a double-breasted suit—something many fashion experts insist shouldn't be done, but Astaire went ahead and did anyway. In this, Astaire perpetrated the demurest of deceptions, just as the famous arbiter of taste Beau Brummell apocryphally confessed in a self-mocking quatrain:

> My neckcloth, of course, forms my principal care,
> For by that we criterions of elegance swear,
> And costs me, each morning, some hours of flurry,
> *To make it appear to be tied in a hurry.*

As the Beau well knew, the amateurs are always trying to look perfect and pressed to the marrow, while the real pros go for the calculated mistake. And instead of that studied attempt at perfection (bound to fail anyway), how much better to appear slightly vague and obfuscating, rather than flaunting that top wattage logo across your chest. Vagueness insures security. ("Where did I buy the shoes? Cobbler fellow made them, some little hovel of a shop in one of those back streets of Budapest, place stunk like a dead water buffalo, absolutely floor-to-ceiling with piles of raw leather.") Showing complete ignorance about the obvious, not knowing one's size, or of what material one's jacket is made is always a good idea. ("They say soldiers at the Somme used this stuff to clean the cannons.") So maddening for others to think you look so well turned out without trying or even knowing anything about it.

"Haven't bought clothes in years" is an almost unbeatable ploy, since any reply would seem rather arriviste and petty at the same time. (Of course this only works well if your clothes are actually beyond the grasp of trendy fashion). I remember the first time I was fed a line like this—to great impression, I might add. I was interviewing a gentleman member of one of Philadelphia's first families (no names please) for an article on formalwear and was foolish enough to ask him where he bought his evening kit. "Oh, Mr. Boyer," he drawled in a perfect, lock-jawed, Main Line accent, "I don't *buy* evening clothes. I *have* evening clothes." Spot on, and leaving me feeling very definitely one down.

Then there's the purposefully incongruent finesse of mixed genres. And credit where credit's due, the Italians have brought this little ploy to perfection, if not actually invented it. The well-worn Barbour jacket over a town suit, or a wonderfully tailored camel-hair polo coat with faded jeans and an old cashmere turtleneck, can be a nicely confusing discernment. Not to mention the inspired oversight of an undone cuff button or that slightly tousled pocket handkerchief or pair of worn bedroom slippers to convey the appropriate subtext that one has responded to the chaos and darkness of the universe with elegant disdain.

The key here, as the Italians know, is to keep the viewer guessing. That bright orange silk pocket square you wore with the navy flannel double-breasted suit came off very dashing, but was it selected with that in mind, or was it just a lucky rushed grab? Or what about that bright Russell plaid sports jacket worn with that equally bright polka dot tie? Eye-scorching mistake or canny bit of upmanship?

Cultivate the impression of never having prepared. A designer friend I happen to know spends considerable time each morning trying on different combinations of gear before venturing out, but never admits to anything but "simply grabbing the top shirt in the drawer." Often it's possible to take a step forward by taking two backwards: trouser braces from some vintage shop, Dad's old fishing vest, a World War I French army officer's great coat, an old garrison belt from a vintage shop. A slightly more advanced twist is something old used in a new way: a vintage cigar case used for eyeglasses, the neglected fishing creel for a briefcase, or an old stud box to carry a few Ativan and aspirin all have the acceptable idiosyncrasy.

To bring this discussion full circle, *sprezzatura* is the grand trompe l'oeil of style in the aesthetics of public life. And it is

perhaps also a solution to the terrible dilemma we've gotten ourselves into, in which the most private aspects of people's lives
are mere grist for the TV confessional mill or website, while
fewer and fewer feel any civic duty and responsibility at all. Perhaps, after so long an absence, we should return to those dusty
etiquette guides and reconsider the idea of the public *occasion*,
when traditionally behavior was considerably different from what
it was behind closed doors. We might even start teaching manners again. And develop a civic style in which a bit of well-placed
artifice and gracefulness can be appreciated. As the eighteenth-
century English poet Alexander Pope so well understood:

> True Ease comes from Art, not Chance,
> *As those move easiest who have learn'd to dance.*

23

SUITS

ON OCTOBER 7, 1666, when Samuel Pepys was a minor official in the British navy, he went to a morning council meeting to hear the day's news and events. There he was witness to a remarkable pronouncement from King Charles II—a declaration that would change the course of fashion history. As Pepys recorded in his diary the next day, "The King hath yesterday in council declared his resolution of setting a fashion for clothes, which he will never alter. It will be a vest, I know not well how. But it is to teach the nobility thrift, and will do good."

The king's declaration came as something of a surprise to Englishmen, who were used to wearing doublets (tight, high-buttoning jackets), breeches (short trousers), and cloaks. What the king proposed, in addition to the vest of which Pepys made note, was a coat and longer breeches. In short, a three-piece suit.

Whether Charles was in the forefront of this fashion trend or merely caught the blowing wind in his sails is not clear, but we do know that the style of dress to which he gave his imprimatur became immediately popular. A week later, on the fifteenth of October, Pepys went to Westminster Hall to see the king in his new finery:

This day the King begins to put on his vest, and I did see several persons of the House of Lords, and Commons too, great courtiers, who are in it—being a long cassocke close to the body, of black cloth and pinked [i.e., slashed] with white silk under it, and a coat over it, and the legs ruffled with black riband like a pigeon's leg—and upon the whole, I wish the King may keep it, for it is a very fine and handsome garment.

Those few weeks in October 1666 mark a turning point in social history. The rigid formality of court dress was on the way out and the swing toward sartorial democracy had begun—a process initiated, ironically enough, by a restored monarch.

It would take another two hundred years before this three-piece outfit became the modern suit we wear today, but the Great Renunciation—the shift away from the gorgeousness of court dress with its silks and satins, silver buckles, and powdered wigs—eventually gave rise to modern worsted suiting, cotton shirts, and the discreet neckwear of the corporate business outfit. In time, the style prescribed in the king's proclamation became a bureaucratic uniform. (See the Introduction for more on the Great Renunciation.)

In the centuries since Charles II's declaration, the styling and proportion of the suit have changed this way and that according to the whims of fashion. The hems of men's coats started to rise perceptively from the knee shortly before the mid-nineteenth century, and continued to move further up the leg until they reached the bottom of the buttocks at the end of the 1860s, where they have more or less remained ever since. Men's trousers had already been cut to fall from waist to ankle by the 1820s, by which time vests had assumed their modern shape as waistcoats. Changes in construction, production, and fashion have been relatively minor ever since. At first this shorter coat was seamed at the waist—called a "frock coat"—with a high-button stance. But by 1850, the lounge jacket and lounge suit had made their tentative appearance: "Being loose and comfortable its popularity steadily increased. Made S-B and slightly waisted, at first just covering the seat, then increasing towards the end of the decade. The fronts hung straight; no seam at the waist or hip buttons or pleats but a short back vent was usual. . . . Closed by three or four buttons." By 1870 the mode of styling this garment was set for the following century and a half.

Since the late nineteenth century, nothing much about the modern suit—including the motivation—has changed. Indeed, this is perhaps the suit's most interesting aspect—particularly when you think how quickly fashions change. As fashion writer and art historian Anne Hollander puts it, "advances in technology and economic organization during the past two centuries have in fact been bent on *preserving* the character of men's tailoring and spreading its availability." The suit is done evolving, in other words, and is now simply conquering as much of the sartorial universe as we'll grant it.

There are only two basic silhouettes of the suit coat: the single-breasted and the double-breasted. Both have been worn with and without a vest. The single-breasted coat has always been the most popular, at least for civilian wear; military uniforms, such as the double-breasted reefer coats of the world's navies, are another matter. The easiest explanation for this choice is that single-breasted coats work best on horseback, but we'll leave that debate to heavier tomes.

Single-breasted suits and sports jackets are in the main distinguished and defined by the front closure: either one, two, three, or four buttons—the last not seem much since the early years of the twentieth century. The three-button coat has been the most popular and arguably most serviceable most of the time. Other details such as breadth of shoulders and width of lapels, waisted or straight silhouette, patch or besom pockets, vented or ventless back are matters of momentary fashion.

The only aspect of the single-breasted suit that seems idiosyncratically cyclic is whether the outfit is comprised of two or three pieces. I'm referring here to that highly functional garment, the

vest. Called a "waistcoat" by British tailors, the vest has actually
risen to the waist in the time since it first became popular in the
1660s as a knee-length undercoat (scholars can date a waistcoat
from its length alone). Originally vests had sleeves, but these
were discarded in the early years of the nineteenth century, and
by the 1840s a tailor's pattern for a vest was pretty much what
it is today: a sleeveless shell with a front six-button closure and
buckled back, front edges pointed or rounded, either two or four
pockets, and with or without lapels.

    The fortunes of the vest have risen and fallen with the vicis-
situdes of fashion and with the relationship of the vest to the
cut of the coat front, the shirt collar, and the importance of the
neckwear. As Shakespeare said, fashion wears out more clothes
than the man.

Whether a suit *should* include a vest or not is more a matter of fashion than practicality—but when it comes to personal tailoring (that is, having a suit made), a vest is undoubtedly a good idea for several reasons. First, it increases the variety of the outfit to provide several looks; second, it provides more pockets; and third, it makes the outfit more responsive to changes in weather. This latter point is particularly important when traveling from one climate to another.

Interestingly enough, good vest makers are always in short supply. There are two reasons for this. First, it's a rather precarious specialty, since one never knows whether vests will be popular at any given moment. And second, because the vest is the tailored garment that sits closest to the skin and must be perfectly smooth, it allows for little leeway. A vest that's too loose or tight is an all too obvious mistake, and an uncomfortable one at that.

Climate-controlled buildings have made wearing a vest with a double-breasted suit superfluous, but not the d-b suit itself. In fact, if you want a dressy suit, you couldn't do better than a double-breasted one. I proffer this tip knowing full well it may cause a few qualms in some of you novices out there. I hope to allay those feelings as we go along.

In some quarters the d-b is just being discovered; in other quarters it never went away. I was reminded of this in 2011, when I attended the auction of the estate of Douglas Fairbanks Jr., the acclaimed American actor, style icon, and son of famed silent film star Douglas Fairbanks Sr. The wardrobe collection contained a dozen double-breasted suits and jackets, three of which were sumptuous d-b cut-velvet dinner jackets. Needless to say, there was considerable interest.

I don't want to rehash the history of the d-b, fascinating though it is; rather, I'd like to consider the myths surrounding the garment, just in case there are any men out there who have never worn a double-breasted suit or jacket before.

Many of us men have the remarkable ability to convince ourselves we have good reasons for doing what we want and not

doing what we're fearful of. The wearing, or rather the *not* wearing of d-b suits, falls into the latter category. Of men's reasons for not wearing d-bs there seems to be no end. What you hear is, "I just can't wear them, not with my figure." Then come the reasons: "I'm too short / heavy / tall / thin / angular [you fill in the category]." As though style had anything to do with physique.

But of course it gets much worse than that, doesn't it? Some men will tell you they can't wear d-bs because there's something about the flap of the coat that makes the eye wander off center, or that the overlap increases both the visual field and the actual bulk of the person, or that the d-b calls attention to itself at the point of the abdomen, etc., etc., etc. One men's style manual I saw recently says something like "the d-b is not for men on the shorter or heavier side as it adds fabric to your midsection," which more or less sums up the idiocy.

There are so many great steaming piles of reasons why people shouldn't wear d-b suits, all of which make about as much sense as, not to put too fine a point on the metaphor, manure from a hobbyhorse. But you only have to look around to see proof of its falsity. Let me give as good an example as I can.

I once met Aristotle Onassis, and I can tell you that physically he was no Cary Grant or Brad Pitt. It struck me at the time that he was more pear-shaped than anything, a bit heavier in the middle and slighter at the shoulders. But he looked about as greatly turned out as anyone I'd ever seen: pristine white silk dress shirt and navy silk tie, highly polished black calf bespoke shoes, and a beautifully cut navy silk double-breasted suit. Accessorized with a blazingly white pocket square and those heavy black eyeglasses for which he was known, he oozed elegance from every pore.

Too many men needlessly forego the pleasures of all sorts of items of the wardrobe, but when it comes to the glories of the d-b, it's a real tragedy. Think of the great dressers of our age: the propitious Prince of Wales and the more dandyesque Alan Flusser, the consummate Italian clothiers Mariano Rubinacci and Luciano Barbera, actors Jude Law and Denzel Washington, and the masterly lifestyle maven Ralph Lauren. All of them come in various shapes and sizes, and all of them are partial to d-bs. This business about the rules, what one can and shouldn't wear, is all a matter of attitude, not physique.

Having said all of that, I suppose there are a few styling tips to keep in mind. The d-b suit is more formal and has more an air of urbanity than its single-breasted brother. Because of this, it's more easily given to solids and stripes than checks (although plaids can look particularly natty in a d-b). Furthermore, by tradition the d-b always takes peak lapels; notch lapels are reserved for single-breasted jackets. Third, the underneath flap of coat front is kept in place with a "jigger" button; this is propriety. And fourth, the coat is usually cut a bit shorter than a single-breasted to compensate for the additional material in the overflap; this is styling.

The classic d-b, whether in a suit coat or blazer, has six buttons, of which two are generally fastened. But this is not a rule, because some men opt to fasten only the bottom right button. And to confuse matters even more, some men prefer only four buttons rather than six, or even only two buttons side by side. This latter approach is usually regarded with suspicion, as diverting too far from the norm. But it's always nice to have options. And stylish men often step over the line a bit.

24

SUMMER FABRICS

A WHILE BACK I WAS LUCKY ENOUGH to be invited
to lunch at Manhattan's famous theatrical establishment the
Players Club. It's since become my favorite place in the world.
Originally a townhouse bought by the esteemed nineteenth-
century American actor Edwin Booth (brother of the not-as-
esteemed actor and Lincoln assassin, John Wilkes Booth), and
remodeled for the club by Belle Epoque superstar architect Stanford White, the place absolutely reeks of stage history, perhaps in
some cases literally, because there are dozens of historical cos-
tumes scattered about on display. There are also death masks of
famous actors, hundreds of wonderful portraits of famous actors
and actresses (including some by John Singer Sargent), and tons
of prop swords, canes, springer daggers, stage furniture, and other
theatrical items. Not to mention one of the best and most agreeable theatrical libraries in the country.

But out of all these attractions, the item that most caught my
eye was in the downstairs restaurant. The Grill Room is a small
dining room with a bar at one end, a fireplace, tables scattered
about, and a billiards table. I asked my host if people ever used
the billiards table. "All the time, since the club was first formed

in 1888," he said. "The pool cue hanging over the fireplace was Mark Twain's."

I sat there eating my turkey club sandwich and thought about that. What a great fin de siècle scene it must have been: Mark Twain shooting pool with a few fellas puffing on Havana cigars, moving their brandy snifters along the cushion to make a carom shot. Stanford White would likely have been one of those men, for he also frequented the Player's Club; indeed he had his last meal there on the balmy evening of June 25, 1906, before going off to Madison Square Garden for a rendezvous with his mistress, the great beauty of the day Evelyn Nesbit, only to be discovered there by Evelyn's husband and shot to death.

Did either White or Harry Thaw wear a linen suit as they shot pool in this very room?, I wondered. Twain, iconoclast that he was, loved white linen suits. He once gave an interview to the *New York Times* in which he commented on his favorite outfit. "I have found," he explained, "that when a man reaches the advanced age of 71 years as I have, the continual sight of dark clothing is likely to have a depressing effect upon him. Light-colored clothing is more pleasing to the eye and enlivens the spirit." A good point, and enlivening the spirit is something we can always use a bit of. A handsome white linen suit won't stabilize the Dow Jones, ease tensions on the Indian subcontinent, or make TV any more interesting. But on the other hand, it might grant its wearer a touch of extra self-esteem, brighten the scenery of which he's a part, and give a lift to his spirits and those of people around him. It's worth considering.

Over the past century, the white suit has been promenaded resplendently in a variety of fabrics: doeskin flannel and twill gabardine, silk shantung, cotton, and even wool barathea. But linen has invariably been the fabric of choice. In the American South, linen was always a sign of respectability. International dandy Tom Wolfe—perhaps the poster boy, after Twain, for the white linen suit—has said his sartorial choices might have been unconsciously influenced by his boyhood in Richmond, Virginia, where "no even halfway proper gentleman went out in the street, no matter how hot it was, without a coat and tie, and there were a lot of white linen suits."

The gentlemen's club, white linen suits, and billiards and brandy have now all but been replaced on our social scene by hyper-designed athletic shoes, high-tech devices, and diet soft drinks. But not quite! Linen has been once again gaining ground as a fabric of choice for suitings and casual wear. I'm putting it down to comfort and elegance, but then those have always been my peculiar touchstones of style. I have a hard time understanding how there could be any other reason for wearing something, but that's just me.

Linen—woven from the fibers of the flax plant (*linum usitatissimum*, if you want the precise botanical name)—has been around longer than civilization and may be our oldest body covering, not counting fig leaves of course. Linen had been woven into garments in Egypt for centuries before the biblical physician Luke told his story of the proper gentleman—"a certain rich man, which was clothed in purple and fine linen, and fared sumptuously every day," and who lived quite a way east of Richmond. It was apparently understood from the very beginning that linen was not only a durable material but capable of being easily cleaned by washing. By the Middle Ages linen had become the principal textile in Europe, not unknown even among the poor. The fabric was used for a variety of purposes, from sheets and shrouds, to napkins and towels, as well as clothing, outerwear and underwear.

In the history of body-worn linen, however, it has been habits of cleanliness that have made the crucial difference. By the seventeenth century people were learning new hygienic modes, which included changing clothes every now and then, and occasionally cleaning them. Linen could be easily cleaned without it being ruined in the process. The facts are recounted fully by Daniel Roche in his fascinating study *The Culture of Clothing*: "the spread of linen, especially shirts, paved the way for the introduction of the more systematic bodily cleanliness of changing."

Fine linen shirting and underwear (called "small linen" at the time) became the standard of upper-class respectability by the mid-eighteenth century. What distinguished the man of quality in appearance was his ability to change his shirt frequently, and it's estimated that even the average French shopkeeper had perhaps six linen shirts, while the more professional and wealthy man had perhaps as many as twenty-five or so. Writer-philosopher Jean-Jacques Rousseau went absolutely bonkers when, after returning home from a concert one night, he discovered that forty-two of his finest linen shirts had been stolen.

Irish, Belgian, and Italian linens have traditionally been the most highly prized, and the wearing of clean linen became one of the features of modern dress. The English naturalist Gilbert White (1720–1793) noted that "the use of linen changes of shirts or shifts, in the room of sordid and filthy woolen, long worn next to the skin, is a matter of neatness, comparatively modern." By the turn of the nineteenth century George "Beau" Brummell became the idol of fashionable London society by building his wardrobe around his personal dress code, in which "very fine linen, plenty of it, and country washing" should accompany a daily bath. Brummell's dictum and advice were rather revolutionary at the time, but eventually taken very seriously by his aristocratic friends of the Regency period. More and more men who could afford it actually started to change their clothes and bathe frequently. Although public sanitation would have to wait a bit longer, our modern standards of personal hygiene began to take shape during his lifetime.

Just as gradually, cotton came to replace much of the linen for shirts and undergarments, but linen was still used for outer garments. At the turn of the twentieth century natives and visitors to sophisticated southern climes—Italy, Cuba, the Southern United States, Spain, Provence—would have encountered plenty of men in white linen suits, heavily starched and pressed. Such treatments wouldn't have kept them from creasing, but that was part of the charm and panache. If anything, linen's rumpled elegance is even more charming in today's age of indestructible synthetic fibers that resemble aluminum foil. What's wanted in linen is nonchalance, that insouciant sangfroid that says you're too cool to care. Perhaps the reverse snobbery was just a tad too obvious when Ralph Lauren found it necessary to insure his less secure customers that his suits were the Real Thing by sewing a "guaranteed to wrinkle" label into them, or when Giorgio Armani had his suits hung on racks straight from the washer. But the connoisseurs of the white linen suit would have needed no reassurance: think Noel Coward at the Casino in Monte Carlo, Gary Cooper poolside in Beverley Hills, possibly even George Clooney at Lake Como, and let us not forget distingué writer Tom Wolfe strolling the Upper East Side of Manhattan.

Of course, it's not only white we're talking about now. Italian men have a particular way with linen, realizing that dress has not been brought down to the level of a science—it remains an art. In my time I've seen both Luciano Berbera and Sergio Loro Piana—two distinguished dressers if there ever were any—in tobacco-brown linen double-breasted suits made, I'm sure, by the great A. Caraceni in Milan; they were absolute poems of the genre. Sand is another tasteful alternative, as is olive, navy, and sage green. And the esteemed Neapolitan Mariano Rubinacci is fond of wearing black linen suits in the evening—very chic indeed. Even pastels are not unheard of with the more boulevardier members of the clan: pink and pale orange and peacock blue, buttery yellow, pearl gray, and mint.

The genre calls for a certain discipline and self-scrutiny; it's not for the faint of heart, the confused, or the timid. In an age when so much of the garment industry continues to tout the wrinkle-free, nonironing properties of polyester, there's romance in the wrinkles of natural linen. They convey the gifts of comfortable decorum, grace, and perfect nonchalance and unconcern, even disdain for those who seek sleek perfection. Wearing a linen suit remains something of an act of confidence, because the gentle creases and folds that accrue must be accepted as a touch of poise, finesse, and natural assurance. Over time the color of fine linen will gently fade a bit and patinate, and patination is a sign that clothes are old friends. This is yet another indication of the triumph of style over regimentality. Perhaps it's not for the aesthetically immature, but for the man of confidence and personal flair, you can't beat linen.

And what of the other cloths of summer? Since the latter decades of the twentieth century or so, much of the attention has been given to the extra-fine merino wools called "super cloths." Cloth innovations such as this were undoubtedly the most exciting development in menswear in the second half of the twentieth century. If there has been one major trend in men's clothing, it's been toward comfort. The actual *wearability* has changed enormously.

Contemplate, if you will, just how excruciatingly uncomfortable most men's clothing was before this shift. For instance, the dark worsted suit typically worn by the businessman of a hundred years ago was made of a heavy cloth that weighed in at between twelve and eighteen ounces per yard, and as high as twenty ounces (a suit normally takes about four linear yards of cloth). This would have been worn along with a highly starched dress shirt, hard felt derby hat, and ankle-high button shoes. In winter he'd add an overcoat of heavy melton cloth (twenty ounces or more). The outfit was dark, stiff, cumbersome, dense, and leaden. There was no air-conditioning, and propriety was such that gentlemen did not remove their jackets in the office. I leave you for a moment to ponder that.

No wonder the thrust of sartorial innovation has been toward comfort. Yet funnily enough, it's not the *styling* that has given us this freedom from being stifled to death by our own clothing, because the style of tailored garments and their appurtenances hasn't changed all that much in the past hundred years and more. Rather, it's the fabric. Technology has provided us with fabrics that are at the same time lightweight, soft, and still durable enough to withstand repeated wearing and cleaning.

Fabric is the essential component of a good suit. Even the best tailor can't make up for poor quality cloth. Traditionally, they've relied upon natural fibers—wool, linen, cotton, silk. Wool has been the standard since the eighteenth century, when during the Great Renunciation (see the Introduction) men turned away from silks and satins and instead concentrated on tailored garments that, in one way or another, reflected the body that wore them. This turn toward practicality first came about in Britain, whose weavers expertly produced woolen cloths for hundreds of years. Wool has many attributes to recommend it: it tailors well, and it breathes, wears well, responds well to cleaning, pressing, and altering. Wool's also hygroscopic, capable of absorbing water in excess of 30 percent of its weight, yet doesn't feel damp because it can quickly shed the moisture, wicking it back into the air. No wonder sheep seem so comfortable in it.

Today, as our environment becomes more and more climate-controlled, we also have lighter-weight, all-season suitings—many of which, strange as it may sound, incorporate wool. Cloth production for the majority of tailored garments still starts with good wool, and undoubtedly the most renowned wool comes from the merino sheep found in Australia and New Zealand. Supple yet amazingly strong, it's considered the wool of choice for superior suiting. The top line of the untreated fleece is bought at auction by cloth producers and shipped to their mills where it's processed: scoured, dyed, carded, and spun into yarn. After that, the yarn is woven into a variety of fabrics: flannels and tweeds, worsteds, gabardines, high-twist plain weaves, twills. The list is long.

Since the beginning of wool weaving, the fleece has been "graded"; that is to say its fineness has been determined—rather subjectively. Experts simply rubbed the fibers between their fingers and estimated how fine it was. That's why the way wool feels is even today usually referred to as "hand," short for "handle." But recently a more scientific system has been devised to accurately measure the grade of the fibers. A fiber of the fleece is measured in microns (a micron is much finer than a human hair) with a sophisticated electron microscope, and the best fibers are designated "superfine." Superfine fibers are thinner yet longer and more resilient. They are so fine that a pound of Super 100s wool—the number refers to the diameter measured in microns, anywhere from fifty to over two hundred—can be spun into a thread thirty miles long. In essence, the higher the super number, the finer the super cloth. Some super fabrics weigh less than eight ounces per linear yard and carry their duties with good crease resistance and draping ability to hold up in heat and humidity.

These super cloths have been getting a lot of attention since the 1980s, but there are other natural-fiber fabrics that should be considered as well. Fresco cloth, for example, is a more traditional worsted cloth that has been popular since the 1920s for summer suiting and remains a great choice. It's a cloth whose yarns have been twisted before being loosely woven. This technique produces a cloth that's crisp but amazingly porous and very wrinkle-resistant. Early frescos suffered from being a bit scratchy and, at about fourteen ounces, were relatively heavy, but since the invention of machinery capable of twisting lighter-weight yarns, the weight of frescos has been greatly reduced. First it was brought down to nine ounces, and just a few seasons ago to a remarkable seven ounces, without losing any of its unique properties of airiness, springy resistance to wrinkles, and slightly pebbled hand. The cloth makes an excellent choice for suits, sports jackets, and odd trousers, particularly for the travel wardrobe.

You wouldn't ordinarily think that cashmere was a warm-weather fabric, and up to about twenty-five years ago you would have been right. Cashmere has traditionally been woven by the "woolens" weaving system, a process used for heavier cloths in which the fibers are not stretched out and combed flat. That's why heavier tweeds and flannels, for example, have a dense, slightly fluffy or spongy hand. The other major method used for weaving wool is called the "worsted" system, and it produces a flatter, smoother weave capable of constructing lighter-weight cloths. But starting after World War II experimentation led to worsted-weaving machinery that was able to deal with the more delicate cashmere fibers, and now virtually every cloth merchant offers cashmeres in the seven-and-a-half-ounce to eight-and-a-half-ounce range. Lightweight cashmere has a wonderfully soft, cloudlike feel and takes color dyes incomparably, so that shades of cashmere look both muted and soft, but vibrant and strong at the same time.

The drawback of lightweight cashmere is its lack of durability and wrinkle resistance. It just doesn't have the mileage that the high-twist fabrics do. Rather too delicate for trousers, the cloth is more appropriate for a special-occasion sports jacket or some such item. This delicate nature can be somewhat mitigated by blending it with other fibers such as silk, wool, or linen. Earlier blended fabrics relied on synthetic fibers woven with cottons and wools, but the current trend is toward all natural combinations that attempt to present the best qualities of each fiber used. This seems to me to be much preferable, not least because natural fibers are better in their ability to breathe. So a blend of cashmere, silk, and wool will have the crease resistance of wool, the low luster of silk, and the softness of cashmere all in a lightweight cloth. The percentage of each fiber used is determined by which properties are most wanted in the fabric.

Besides the mixture of cashmere, silk, and wool, another good summer fabric blend is mohair and silk. Both of these materials have an elegant, urbane air about them, both a slight luster. And both have been making something of a comeback. Not since Frank Sinatra, Dean Martin, Sammy Davis Jr., and the rest of the Rat Pack were seen on stage at the Sands Casino in Las Vegas in the late 1950s and early '60s has mohair looked so masculinely sexy as it does in today's narrow suits. Laser-cut silhouettes are perfect for this urbane fabric, and today it's even better than it was when the Pack made it popular.

Formerly the fibers in mohair came from mature angora goats. Long and stiff, these fibers had a high luster, slightly abrasive hand, and somewhat brittle structure, which meant the fabric was a bit scratchy and shiny, with a tendency to split along the creases. Today's mohair fabric is woven of fleece combed from young goats—therefore called "kid" mohair—and is finer and softer, with a lower luster. Many of the cloth mills that weave the fabric blend it with just a touch of fine merino wool, which enhances these properties and makes the material more durable in the bargain. Because mohair presents colors with such a depth of jewellike clarity—aubergine, black, midnight blue, burnt umber brown, and charcoal gray are favored shades—evening wear and city suits are considered more appropriate than country clothes for the fabric.

Silk is often blended with mohair, as it is with wool. Like mohair, it has a touch of luster. Like another warm-weather fabric, linen, it is ancient. If you want to know about the origins of the product, I suggest you consult a biology text devoted to the various insects involved, especially moth caterpillars, and the process of excreted viscous fluids of protein filaments from various ducts, glands, and spinnerets. It's all a bit too sensational for me.

As far as human history is concerned, at least, silk fabric is a long story, one wrapped in myth and legend. Its history intersects with the tale of—and gives its name to—the famed Silk Road, the trade route that stretched from China to the Mediterranean. It's a colorful history, one stretching back roughly four thousand years and filled with traders and merchants, pilgrims and soldiers, emperors and thieves.

It's thought that silk culture first came to the West via Constantinople between 500 and 600 CE, and that by the fourteenth century Italy had already gained a reputation for producing fine silk fabric. Today, Western countries no longer produce much silk, but Italian mills still produce limited quantities of the fabric—particularly those variants referred to as "raw," of which

shantung and *doppione* are the best known. Shantung, a rougher
silk, has been used more for accessories such as neckwear and
hat bands, but *doppione* enjoyed something of a stylish trend in
the 1950s for elegant suits and eveningwear. Its reputation as
a fashionable look was given a boost when Sinatra and friends
became aficionados, appearing on stage in glimmering silk tuxedos and suits of knife-edged precision cut by Beverly Hill's tailor and haberdasher Sy Devore. Slim, shimmering, and pristinely
elegant, this look captured the laid-back confidence and sleek
sophistication of the urban scene at the time. It was equal parts
L.A. cool, Vegas hip, and Continental chic. Many have said it
was America's finest hour as far as men's style is concerned: perfectly cut lustrous suits, sparkling white shirts with rounded pin
collars and lots of cuff showing, silver satin ties, straw fedoras
with broad silk bands, brightly colored pocket puffs, and shined
slip-ons. You can see it all in the 1960 Rat Pack film *Ocean's
Eleven*.

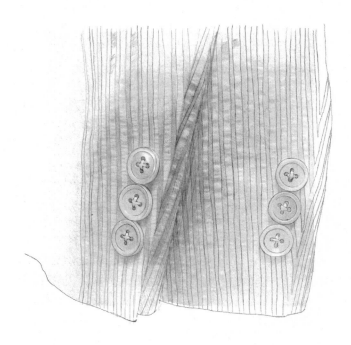

At the other end of the summer fabric spectrum is seer-sucker. This most-recognized of summer suiting fabrics, with its alternating rough and smooth stripes, was probably first woven in India. (The name "seersucker" is a Hindi corruption of a Persian phrase *shir shaker*, which translates as "milk and sugar.") This etymology might explain the differing textures that make up the stripes in the fabric. Seersucker's distinctive feature, these stripes are achieved by what is called slack-tension weaving, in which alternating groups of fibers are held under normal tension while the intervening ones are kept slack; the resulting fabric has an intrinsic, and peculiarly distinct, pattern of puckered and flat stripes.

Garments made of seersucker are by their very nature rumpled, which makes ironing superfluous. This is not only seer-sucker's most distinctive characteristic, but its greatest virtue as well. One doesn't worry about wrinkles because the stuff is permanently wrinkled, which, when it comes to warm weather wear, presents a solution near genius.

Seersucker fabric was first used in the American South as inexpensive and utilitarian clothing, only reaching Northern cities as popular suiting in the 1920s. To understand why, it's worth delving into a bit of sociology, since the appeal of seersucker has much to do with its wrinkly nature.

We could say (as some surely do) that unwrinkled clothing represents some sort of aesthetic ideal based primarily on concerns of hygiene, and that wrinkled clothing bespeaks a slovenly person. But unwrinkled clothes are also interpreted as a symbol of wealth, as they suggest that the wearer is above manual labor. Promoting wrinkle-free clothing therefore caters to this latter idea and represents an auxiliary part of the white-collar syndrome that took hold in the wake of the Industrial Revolution and predominated with the rise of the middle class. The idea of conspicuous consumption—as laid out with great clarity and humor in the great American sociologist Thorstein Veblen's *Theory of the Leisure Class*, first published in 1899—can be aptly applied here. Women in huge skirts with bustles and men in wrinkle-free clothes say the same thing: "I don't have to do any physical work."

It's easy to see what Veblen would have made of inexpensive, wrinkle-free synthetic fibers. Their relatively recent invention has meant that a noncorrugated appearance is no longer a goal, since almost anyone—no matter how strapped—can afford the look. Technology has, in short, made it necessary to change the aesthetic rules of fashion, even though the underlying principle remains the same.

Seersucker is, to state the obvious, at the opposite end of the spectrum from such space-age, wrinkle-free fabrics. Until the 1920s, seersucker was still considered work-clothes-type material. In the 1930s Brooks Brothers sold seersucker suits for fifteen dollars. But then university men began to take it up, and it gained status rapidly, first on campus, then at the country club. Today a quality, pure-cotton, decently made seersucker suit is no longer an inexpensive item (although there are less expensive ones blended with polyester). But this natty and comfortable-as-hell garment remains the monarch of summer suiting—a material that puts all wools, mohairs, and (yes) even linens to shame.

25

TURTLENECKS

TURTLENECK SWEATERS ARE—or at least should be—a default item with tailored clothing in cooler weather. A turtleneck sweater with a suit? Why not? Purposeful nonchalance of this sort has its place. In the 1920s the then Prince of Wales took to wearing turtlenecks with sports jackets and with plus fours for golf. In the '30s and '40s, Hollywood stars like Robert Taylor, Douglas Fairbanks Jr., Errol Flynn, and others wore both suits and sports jackets with turtleneck and polo-collared sweaters—a semi-casual approach that seems to have been invented in California, of all places.

Back then the turtleneck had an added panache of toughness, but that's the thing about the turtleneck: for most of its life it's had a variety of associations—evoking either a hearty out-of-doors laborer or sportsman, or an intellectual, or a criminal. These categorizations may strike you as strange, but let me explain.

Like most modern menswear, this sweater (called a "roll neck" by many Brits) started off as a perfectly utilitarian garment: a heavy-scoured, natural-hued, wool pullover worn by Irish Aran fishermen and others who made their livelihoods on the high seas. The knitting patterns peculiar to each island family are thought to have been devised to identify the drowned.

From there the turtleneck graduated to the world of leisure sports. In the 1880s it was associated with the fad for bicycling, tennis, yachting, and polo. The *Saturday Evening Post*, America's most popular magazine in the early years of the twentieth century, was fond of showing handsome, square-jawed college students in sporting gear on their covers, like the J. C. Leyendecker drawings of Harvard oarsmen wearing thick-ribbed turtleneck letter sweaters in college colors. An example of the scholar-sportsman.

After World War I, increased interest in outdoor sports added to the list hunting and fishing, skiing, sailing, riding, and an absolute mania for hiking. The hiker's uniform dress: a beret, open-neck shirt, washable khaki shorts, turtleneck sweater, and waterproof rucksack. While the turtleneck is readily seen in sports portraiture of the times, perhaps nothing captures the symbol as well as the famous Hemingway portrait by Yosuf Karsh, actually taken in the 1950s: the straight-on head shot has him looking very much the modern Viking adventurer, all bushy beard and ruggedly hefty turtleneck. Which is exactly how Hemingway wanted to be seen.

This utilitarian aspect never left the turtleneck in fact or symbol. Many World War II sailors who fought the Battle of the North Atlantic were terribly glad for their thick wool turtlenecks, watch caps, and thick peacoats during long, dark, penetratingly cold nights on deck. We see them in our memory's eye at the rail, the dark top of the sweater peeking out from the peacoat, binoculars slung 'round the neck. I remember my uncle, at the time a sailor assigned to a mine sweeper in the North Atlantic, in just such a uniform.

But while the turtleneck has retained these wholesome connotations of hard work and dutifulness and all that, the sweater has also symbolically split into two other camps. On the one hand, it came to be associated closely with what used to be

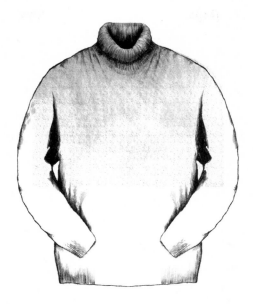

called the criminal classes: the upper-story guys who, in classic detective thrillers of book and film, wore checked-cloth caps, black masks, and dark turtlenecks. All they would have needed to complete the caricature would have been a large canvas bag with "swag" stamped on it. They were eventually caught by the likes of Raffles and Bulldog Drummond, the Saint, the Falcon, and Boston Blackie.

On the other, more genteel and fashionable side of the street, the turtleneck came to be associated with a vein of aesthetes. Evelyn Waugh, up from London to visit his old haunts, went to a party at Merton College, Oxford, on a Saturday evening in November 1924 and recorded the new style in his diary: "Everyone was wearing a new sort of jumper with a high collar rather becoming and most convenient for lechery because it dispenses with all unromantic gadgets like studs and ties. It also hides the boils with which most of the young men seem to have encrusted their necks." A few weeks later Waugh bought himself a turtleneck, although he noted he didn't like himself in it.

Elsewhere, the turtleneck-wearing aesthetes were of a different stamp altogether. Post–World War II French existential bohemians (such as Samuel Beckett, who took up the turtleneck not long after Waugh put it down) and US beatniks made the black turtleneck sweater a part of their daily outfit—an outfit that, in the French case, involved a long black leather jacket à la Jean Paul Sartre and Albert Camus, and that in the American case included variously berets, goatees, jeans, army surplus khaki trousers and field jackets, dark glasses, and bongo drums (see numerous photos of James Dean, Marlon Brando, et al.). Steven Watson's study of the Beat generation includes a wonderful photo of a young William Burroughs standing in an alley outside of his home in Tangier (which he called the Villa Delirium, "the original anything goes joint"), wearing most of the requisite gear, including the prerequisite black turtleneck sweater.

The bohemian and beatnik look was, in fact, only a slightly extreme version of what many university students—many of them ex-soldiers—in the United States and Europe were wearing every day to their classes: army-navy surplus khakis, duffle coats, and turtleneck sweaters. At France's Sorbonne, New Wave bohemianism dictated the black leather jacket de rigueur, as postwar existentialism expressed itself sartorially as antifashion among highly educated youths. In Britain, the baggy and oversized turtleneck became a symbol of the young intellectual, the "angry young men" at redbrick universities, worn with wide-wale corduroys and thick brogues. The outfit was intended to show rebellion against the conservative power structure represented by a tailored wardrobe of dark suit, white shirt, and club tie, as well as solidarity with blue-collar workers as the New Left began to emerge in the West in the mid-1960s.

These "prole" styles were obviously easy to imitate, caricature, and to some extent co-opt. And fashion of course co-opts
everything. As the fascination with turtlenecks moved up the
class ladder, the medium became dressier. More luxurious versions in fine velours and silks were worn by aspiring playboys;
surely Hugh Heffner could not have burned all of those photos
of himself in silk turtlenecks with the short-lived Nehru jackets of the mid-1960s (named after Indian prime minister Jawa-
harlal Nehru, who wisely—if ironically—tended to ignore the
odd-looking, semimilitaristic jacket, which—also ironically—
tended to look better on Nehru than others). An additional bit
of bizarrie was the string of beads that appeared around the
necks of turtleneck sweaters during this time and that echoed
the missing tie—presumably making the many middle-class men
who wore them feel a bit hippie-ish but still safe. These sweaters
differed from their existential brothers in that they were skinny,
body-hugging silhouettes sold in boutiques alongside safari suits,
flowered shirts, and bell-bottomed trousers.

The unfortunate but quickly passing Nehru fad was followed
by the Great Blazer Craze of the 1960s. Wasp-waisted, double-
breasted, navy-blue blazers with deep side vents and shiny metallic crested buttons, which ran down the front like a landing
strip, were paired with white turtlenecks (again, in fine cotton
or silk). The trend was associated with and ascribed to Ant-
ony Armstrong-Jones, a chic photographer who became Lord
Snowden when he married Britain's Princess Margaret in 1960.
As a couple, they were the darlings of London's new swinging set,
ricocheting from one party to the next in their purposefully prole
Mini Cooper. Hoards of men during the period could be found
at gatherings on both sides of the Atlantic wearing this outfit,
looking oddly reminiscent of German U-boat commanders.

Its proletarian origins make the turtleneck one of the first
modern garments to have effectively reversed the route to popularity that men's clothing had traditionally taken. Historically,
styles have always trickled down from the affluent to those below.

What appears to have happened in the case of the turtleneck is that styles gushed up from the street to the penthouse. Jeans and flannel shirts, military parkas and work boots have followed the same path in the intervening years.

But this *nostalgie de la boue* isn't quite so new either. Periods of studied negligence have happened before. Seventeenth-century English Cavaliers were quite consciously nonchalant in their dress (carefully recorded in the painting of Van Dyke and the poetry of Robert Herrick), as had been sixteenth-century German aristos who purposefully slashed their doublets (like some do with their jeans today) to expose the stuffing beneath. Postrevolutionary France, the English Regency era, and Jacksonian America were all periods of intentional dressing down.

So the street tough and the aesthete are not so far apart after all. I believe it was George Orwell who made the point that Evelyn Waugh's university confreres quite literally poured as much beer down their throats as they could, calling it ale as they thought working men did. The Beats and their spiritual flower-power sons of the 1970s were similar in that they took drugs that had first cropped up in poor black neighborhoods in America's inner cities, and played folk songs and the blues to identify with the common man at the bottom of the ladder. *Plus ça change, mes amis, plus c'est la même chose, n'est-ce pas?*

26

WEATHER GEAR

IF THERE'S ONE GARMENT THAT REFLECTS a real shift
in the way we think about clothing in the twenty-first century,
it's the rugged outdoor jacket—the principal piece of weather
gear in most men's closets. For much of the twentieth century,
outerwear was designed with either sport or military outfitting in
mind, or was for the businessman (and thus designed to be worn
over tailored clothing and was itself tailored). But now these former types of outerwear—the military parka, the field-and-stream
coat, the workman's jacket, the explorer's and adventurer's outerwear—make up the majority of the latter category, as well.

Regardless of styling, these military- or sporting-derived outer
garments are characterized by an active ruggedness and have several telling points: (1) They're made of utility fabrics such as heavy
canvas or nylon, rough leather, waxed cotton, melton or boiled
wools, and a variety of natural and synthetic blends. (2) Many
are lined with goose down, blanketing, synthetic insulation, and
quilted zip-in vests. (3) Often they have hoods, of which some
are detachable or concealed. And (4) all of them seem to have
dozens of pockets of every conceivable size and shape. There
are countless possible combinations of these different options,

which might explain why the outdoor jacket has proliferated the way it has. One recent season I noticed that a single designer, Ralph Lauren, was offering a total of 198 outerwear jacket models, including a variety of bomber jackets, trucker jackets, officer's coats, peacoats, biker jackets, duffel coats, pilot's jackets, and ranch coats.

This movement away from tailored garments to rugged casual jackets nicely reflects art historian James Laver's theory that modern menswear begins as either sports or military clothing and then moves into daily life, becoming more and more formal as time goes by, eventually hardening into costume. He cites the tailcoat as an example of this evolution. The tailcoat was, in the early years of the nineteenth century, a fox hunting habit, but by the turn of the twentieth century it had reached the highest formality as evening dress. Today it's worn on only the most formal of occasions and by orchestra conductors, and few tailors even know how to make a set of tails anymore.

I want to get back to Laver's theory in a paragraph or three, but for now I'd point to either the trench coat or the polo coat as good examples of it in outerwear. The polo coat started out as a loosely belted, bathrobe-like garment thrown over the shoulders by polo players to keep warm between periods of play and then was taken up by dashing young men as an everyday coat. Similarly, the trench coat was invented for British officers during the First World War, and the survivors kept it as a practical coat when they were demobilized. Both coats are now considered perhaps not yet formal, but dressy enough to wear over virtually any outfit a man may choose, including a tuxedo.

The trench coat is also, of course, the classic military outer garment taken into civilian use. The original model is still with us a century after the massive trench warfare campaigns of the Great War, as are numerous other "fashion" variations, and as protection from the elements, particularly rain, it has yet to be surpassed. All of which only goes to show that when something is designed well and has practical application, it has staying power.

The main difference in raincoats is not so much a matter of style, which is what most people notice first, but rather of fabric. There are two methods of producing rain-resistant fabric from which the garments are made. Both these methods are still in use today to produce raincoats, and both are to be recommended; it's more a matter of taste than function, really. (It should be noted too that there are less expensive raincoats and parkas made of nylon, which are meant to be folded away when not in use. These are wonderful for travel, very portable, but do not constitute a business coat—or elegant attire in any sense, really—in any case but emergencies.)

The first, slightly older method of producing water-resistant fabric is to bond a layer of rubber to a layer of cotton. This method was discovered by the Scotsman Charles Macintosh (1766–1843—and not to be confused with Charles Rennie Mackintosh, the Scottish architect and painter) in the early 1820s. Macintosh was a chemist by trade and got it into his head to experiment with the concept of rubberized fabric. With many pubs north of the River Tweed called the Highlandman's Umbrella, it isn't surprising that the idea of protection from rain would hold a persistent place in the Scottish mind, but Macintosh seems to have been particularly obsessed. To shorten a story that only chemists find thrilling in detail, he finally perfected a method of bonding a layer of rubber between two layers of cloth.

According to *The Encyclopedia of Clothing and Fashion*, Macintosh described his invention as "'India rubber cloth,' whereby the texture of hemp, flax, wool, cotton, and silk and also leather, paper, and other substances may be rendered impervious to water and air. It was made as a 'sandwich' of two pieces of material surrounding a core of rubber softened by naptha." Coats with this bonded fabric soon became synonymous with rainwear, so much so that even today in Britain a raincoat is commonly referred to as a "mac," and there's a famous Mackintosh brand of rainwear manufacturing in Britain today. These coats, because of the interior layer of rubber, are heavier, stiffer, and less porous— which is why many are made with vents (usually a series of small holes actually) under the arms, so the coat can "breathe," but the water resistance is outstanding.

The other genius of the early years of rainwear—and the inventor of the other, most noble rain-resistant fabric—was Thomas Burberry (1835–1926). Born and educated in a small village in Surrey, he first learned the rudiments of the fabric trade as an apprentice to a country draper and then in 1856 opened his own shop in Basingstoke, Hampshire. With the help of a neighboring cotton mill owner, he began to experiment and eventually hit on a combination process that proved decidedly successful in waterproofing cotton fabric by treating it in both the yarn stage and the fabric stage with lanolin (a purified sheep's wool grease): the cotton yarn was chemically saturated and then tightly woven into fabric, and finally the whole woven piece of fabric was saturated again, which resulted in a waterproofed cloth that was much lighter and cooler than rubberized fabric, with a natural breathability and extremely good water resistance.

Burberry began to specialize in manufacturing and selling by using his "proofed" cloth to make durably protective garments

for field sports—of which he himself was something of an aficionado—and as he became more and more successful, moved
his shop to London in 1891. (The Burberry flagship store was
at Number 30 The Haymarket for about a hundred years, but
is now located at 121 Regent Street.) There he designed and
sold all sorts of outerwear: shooting capes with ingenious pivot
sleeves, riding coats with hidden pleats, a loosely cut "duster"
coat for the new sport of motoring, and many other models besides. The polar explorers Robert Falcon Scott, Ernest Shack-
leton, and Roald Amundsen all wore windproof and waterproof
suits designed and made by Burberry. Even the tents Amundsen
took with him were made by the firm.

In the first decade of the twentieth century, Burberry instituted
a uniform department to design and manufacture cotton military
raincoats. One of these patterns became the famous trench coat
of World War I. The coat was designed to withstand the various
miseries of trench warfare. Its success was assured when it was re-
ported that Lord Kitchener, the famous field marshal and secretary
of state for war, wore one (and was in fact said to be wearing one
in June 1916, when the ship he was on struck a German mine and
all hands were drowned). During those hostilities of 1914–1918,
half a million British soldiers wore Burberry trench coats and other
rain gear. They weren't bullet-proof, but they did offer formidable
protection from rain, wind, cold, and mud.

For such stout service, the years have been good to the re-
doubtable trench coat. It served in World War II and was the
go-to coat for private detectives in noir films of the '40s; Joel
McCrea in *Foreign Correspondent*, Dick Powell in *Murder, My
Sweet*, Robert Mitchum in *Farewell My Lovely*, Alan Ladd in *This
Gun for Hire*, and Humphrey Bogart in *Casablanca* come to mind
immediately. The trench coat seemed to have been eclipsed for
a while by the straight-hanging balmacaan raincoat but has re-
bounded and today can be found in almost every designer collection. Apart from subtle changes in length to suit the fashion
of the times, the trench coat has retained its battle-ready status:

double-breasted, waterproofed khaki cotton, with epaulets, wrist straps to tighten against the wind and rain, a storm shoulder flap and back yoke, wedge back pleat, large collar and throat latch, and reinforced belt complete with metal D-rings (which were originally meant to hold military necessities: water bottle, combat knife, hand grenades, map case, that sort of thing). You probably wouldn't use them for that in downtown Cleveland or San Francisco, but these loops can still be pressed into service as a fine place to hang a camera or travel umbrella.

Just as the classic trench coat is the perfect example of a military garment being pressed into civilian service, the Barbour jacket is the ideal example of a sports garment being taken into general use. Today there are many versions of this coat, every designer has at least one version in his collection, and labels proliferate with imitations. But Barbour makes the original and still the best. (Actually there are three versions of this coat that have gained popularity: the shorter Beaufort and Bedale versions and the Border jacket, a slightly longer style. But these are actually only the three most popular models out of dozens Barbour has developed over the years for sport and for the British military.)

John Barbour (1849–1918) was a Scotsman from Galloway who left the family farm at the age of twenty to test his fortunes as a traveling draper in England. He eventually must have gotten tired of traveling, because in 1894 he settled down and opened a shop in the growing port of South Shields, selling oilskins to a growing community of sailors and fishermen. Within a few years his business became the largest supplier of these outdoor garments, worn not only by sea men but by farmers and other outdoor laborers as well.

From there the Barbour company went on to make uniforms for the military, including the famous Ursula suit worn by Captain George Phillips and his crew on the *Ursula*, one of the first U-class submarines in World War II, and for British international motorcycle teams, Olympic equestrians, royalty, and outdoorsmen everywhere.

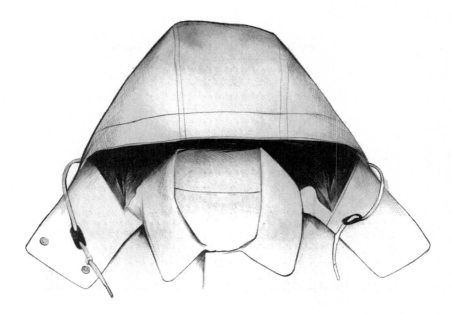

What has made these jackets so popular is their ability to withstand a good deal of wind and rain while keeping the wearer warm and dry. Rather than the "bonded" approach (where rubber is sandwiched between layers of cotton), the Barbour technique is to use Egyptian cotton impregnated with a paraffin-based wax. The advantages are that the fabric is both breathable and supple; the disadvantage is that the cloth must be rewaxed from time to time. Barbour is probably the only clothing company in the world that provides maintenance service for its clothing. Many owners return their coats to South Shields to be reproofed, repaired, or altered.

So the Barbour business didn't accrue from sport and military clothing, as Laver's theory would have it, but rather evolved into it from making workingmen's protective gear. Prole gear is a category apparently not considered by Laver, perhaps because he simply didn't live long enough to see the rise of what we might call "work style." (Laver died in 1975, at which point the wearing of prole gear was a phenomenon still in its infancy and isolated to college campuses, hippie communes, and dude ranches). The Laver theory states that modern menswear starts out as sportswear or military gear and then formalizes. The reality, since roughly mid-twentieth century, has been that men's clothing styles have started at the bottom of the social ladder and then moved upwards, rather than from the top down, as had happened for centuries.

Can these two ideas be squared somehow? I'm not sure. But I do know that there's no better example of an outdoor garment making the journey from prole uniform to designer chic than the lowly ranch jacket. Related to but differing from the barn-style jacket, which covers the hips, the ranch jacket is cut at the waist (and thus is also missing the large lower front pockets found on the barn jacket). This item began humbly enough, but after the hippie-peacock revolution took hold with college students and then moved up the social ladder in the 1960s and '70s, there were examples of aristos having their distressed denim ranch jackets lined in mink—a phenomenon that reminds me of something else that Laver said, which was that the Edwardian Age was the last period in which wealthy people could show off their wealth for the enjoyment of the masses. He obviously predated Kim Kardashian and Kanye West.

The requisite research on the history of the ranch jacket has not yet been done, but presumably the item's origins are in the nineteenth century, along with that other great piece of Western attire, jeans (see Chapter 6). We know that Levi Strauss founded his company to make denim pants in 1853, that he and Jacob Davis patented the classic design (US Patent #139.121) in 1873, and that jeans have remained pretty much the same ever since. Most likely the denim ranch jacket finds its birth sometime between then and the opening years of the twentieth century. What is certain is that the popularity of jeans and the ranch jacket have grown in tandem ever since the rise of the Western film as a genre in the 1920s and the rise of the dude ranch as a vacation resort in the 1930s. By the 1950s the ranch jacket had taken the further step toward its now iconic position by gaining status as the favorite jacket of prole hipsters, completing the basic wardrobe of jeans, T-shirt, and engineer boots. Today, virtually every designer who does a casual collection includes this model in one form or another.

Like its cousin, the black leather motorcycle jacket, the ranch jacket is cut off at the waist and has set-in sleeves and a turndown collar. But unique to the ranch jacket are its two sets of pockets—one patch-and-flap, the other slash—button cuffs, and a button front. For cooler weather it can be lined in cotton flannel. It has a basic utility about it, which is exactly what makes it so susceptible to experimentation. The simple design of the ranch jacket, with its stylistic ability to accompany any sort of trouser, is easy to interpret in virtually any fabric: rough and luxury leathers, exotic skins, expensive furs, satins, synthetics, and of course wools, linens, and silks. A fuchsia crocodile skin ranch jacket is not beyond the realm of the imagination.

More than protecting the lonely cowboy rounding up cattle on the Santa Fe Trail, these jackets have been decorated ad infinitum. Bikers tear off the sleeves, while country singers add embroidery. Nashville's renowned designer and tailor Manuel produced a tour de force in this genre by hand-sewing fifty jackets, one for each state, complete with the individually appropriate state seal, bird, and flower. They are truly works of art and show what can be done with a humble garment when an artist takes command.

Meanwhile, the classic ranch jacket, whether it's made by Levi's or another jeans manufacturer, has held its own, remaining unchanged for a century: waist-length with a six-button front and small turndown collar, button cuffs and buttoned waist tabs, two buttoned chest pockets and two slash side pockets. The fabric is eleven-ounce denim, the buttons are metal with a metal shank, and the orange-colored thread is heavy duty. Anything else is ornament.

The best outdoor jackets and raincoats, of course, only go so far in offering protection from the elements. What about other options, not to mention more practical considerations? What should we be wearing for inclement weather in order to protect ourselves from the nastier elements and still look decent, or even a bit elegant?

Granted, many of us don't spend much time out in the elements the way people used to. These days many people go from their homes to their attached garages, drive to work and park in the underground lot, take an elevator to their office, and then repeat the trip in reverse at day's end. You imagine that some people may not have actually been out of doors in decades. Still, once in a while we need to venture out, and sometimes it's for longer—or in worse weather—than even the sturdiest Barbour, balmacaan, or Macintosh can withstand on its own.

In such instances, there are two basic pieces of foul weather gear to consider. For especially rainy days, umbrellas still seem essential. Like raincoats, they come in too many models and styles to mention and in a variety of materials. But the general rule that quality counts is even more important here because we're dealing with utilitarian concerns, not mere aesthetics. What I'm getting at is that cheap umbrellas are actually very expensive; they don't do the job, and we end up throwing them away rather quickly. Invest in quality: a good umbrella can last for years.

Umbrellas have in fact been around for at least three thousand years, as either rain or sun ("parasols") protectors, and their canopies have been made of everything from paper and lace to silk, cotton gingham, and embroidered satin. Today the best umbrellas have either a metal or wood shaft, and the canopy is made of tightly woven nylon and sometimes of waxed cotton. Black is no longer the only color option. The handle can be made of anything and often determines the price of the umbrella. Traditional handles are wooden, either whangee cane, malacca, or some other hard wood; leather-covered handles are usually more expensive, as are carved wood, crystal, or metals. If you want a real education in the subject, the leading umbrella company in the world is James Smith & Sons in London (53 New Oxford Street), which has been making fine umbrellas, walking sticks, and seat sticks since 1830. The firm carries the largest selection of these items and will do custom orders as well.

Besides umbrellas, proper footwear is the other must when weather turns foul. In such instances, the boot is man's best friend (see Chapter 2), but of course there will be occasions—board meetings and weddings and the like—when it simply won't do to go clomping around indoors in your Bean boots or weather-proofed Fryes.

In such instances, galoshes should be worn over one's dress shoes and removed at the first opportunity once the destination is reached. Easy to slip on and off, these rubber overshoes can be easily balled up, tucked into a plastic bag, and stored in a briefcase or even the pocket of an overcoat. No one will be the wiser—but you, dear reader, will be much the drier.

There are also the more urban rubber shoe covers, diminutive versions of galoshes that only cover part of the shoe. These shoe covers come in various styles and colors (although black is traditional) and are more portable than the heavier galosh. They should be lightweight, skid resistant, and slip off and on easily.

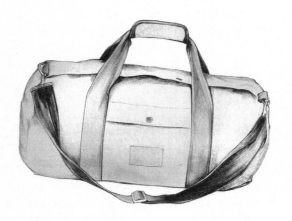

ACKNOWLEDGMENTS

Some of these pieces appear here for the first time, and some appear in altered versions of pieces originally published in the following venues:

ASuitableWardrobe.com
Boyer, G. Bruce. *Elegance: A Guide to Quality in Menswear.* New York: Norton, 1985
Boyer, G. Bruce. *Eminently Suitable: The Elements of Style in Business Attire.* New York: Norton, 1990
Ivy-Style.com
L'Uomo Vogue
MrPorter.com
The Rake

For his significant contributions to this book, Alex Littlefield deserves special thanks. His wise opinions, editing skills, and enthusiasm for this project have made the work a pleasure. His loving and mastery attention to details big and small have guided me at every turn.

I must also acknowledge my indebtedness to Patricia Mears, Deputy Director of the Museum of the Fashion Institute of Technology, for her support and discerning counsel.

APPENDIX:
THE BEST FASHION BOOKS
FOR MEN

**An Idiosyncratic List for the Person Who
Simply Wants to Learn More About Men's Clothes**

Since the 1980s a growing number of fashion books have been devoted to men's clothing, correlating with the rise and importance of menswear designers in the marketplace. Some of these books are serious academic studies, while others are popular histories, lavish coffee-table tomes, advice manuals, and rule books on grooming and dress. Several are a combination of these approaches. Some are silly beyond the imagination; others so erudite the average brain, nay the whole body, boggles trying to decipher them. And some are in that wonderful middle ground, where academic writing becomes accessible to the uninitiated and popular thought takes on a balanced seriousness and wit.

My eighteen shelves of fashion-related books are groaning, and I really should simply abandon many of them—those volumes that should never have been written in the first place, or those I've read but for which I'll never find a use and will never pick up again. But here, in cowardly alphabetical order, are the ones from which I've derived great pleasure and, hopefully, some understanding.

Antongiavanni, Nicholas. *The Suit: A Machiavellian Approach to Men's Style*. New York: Collins, 2006.
A practical guide for the tailored wardrobe and how it should be worn, using the stylistic model of that famous Italian Renaissance treatise *The Prince*. The advice puts rather too much weight on rules and formulas at the expense of creativity and the changes in fashion that time occasions, and thus is necessarily a bit outdated, but the information remains solid and consistent within its own parameters.

Bell, Quentin. *On Human Finery*. 2nd ed., revised and enlarged. New York: Schocken Books, 1976.
A wonderfully well-written study of the Thorstein Veblen theory of conspicuous consumption in Western society as it applies to fashion. This is a serious examination of the subject, but written with wit and entertaining insight for both the historian and the general reader. Bell himself was an artist and member of the Bloomsbury Group—he was Virginia Woolf's nephew—and thus has considerable insight into created finery.

Boyer, G. Bruce. *Elegance: A Guide to Quality in Menswear*. New York: Norton, 1985.
A collection of easily read essays in encyclopedic form on the classics of the male wardrobe, by yours truly. The more service-oriented aspects of the book—lists of shops and purveyors of clothing, for example—are outdated, but the author warned the publisher about this at the start, and now he feels pretty much like Cassandra.

Breward, Christopher, ed. *Fashion Theory: The Journal of Dress, Body & Culture*, vol. 4, no. 4, *Masculinities*. Oxford: Berg, 2000.
A volume of the prestigious *Fashion Theory* journal devoted to masculine fashion, edited by a renowned scholar in the field, and containing incisive essays on tailoring, dress in the 1930s, Hollywood costume, and trends in the second half of the twentieth century.

Carter, Michael. *Fashion Classics from Carlyle to Barthes*. Oxford: Berg, 2003.
A handy one-volume, serious discussion and analysis of the most important fashion texts of the nineteenth and twentieth centuries, from Thomas Carlyle's *Sartor Resartus* to the important work of French cultural critic and literary theorist Roland Barthes.

Chenoune, Farid. *A History of Men's Fashion.* **Translated by Deke Dusinberre. Paris: Flammarion, 1993.**
An excellent history of men's dress in Europe and the United States from 1760 to 1990. The lavish illustrations alone are worth the price of the book. There is a refreshing emphasis on French fashion during this period, and Mr. Chenoune is indeed the expert here.

De Buzzaccarini, Vittoria. *Men's Coats.* **Modena, Italy: Zanfi Editori, 1994.**
This study of the coat is one volume of *The Twentieth Century Fashion Series,* a set of monographs devoted to a discussion of various garments from the end of the nineteenth century to the present. Examples and illustrations are taken mainly from the leading men's magazines of France, Britain, and Italy at the time.

Elms, Robert. *The Way We Wore: A Life in Threads.* **New York: Picador, 2005.**
A lovingly written memoir of a four-decade personal wardrobe journey—1965 to 2005—by an award-winning British journalist, which serves to catalogue virtually every trend of each of those periods in tender and very funny detail. A small treasure that deserves to become a classic.

Flusser, Alan. *Dressing the Man: Mastering the Art of Permanent Fashion.* **New York: HarperCollins, 2002.**
Any of Alan Flusser's books is worth reading, and this one is the most recent, inclusive, and handsome. No one knows more about the practicalities of correct dress than the author, whose advice over the years has been a guiding light for so many well-dressed men.

Fussell, Paul. *Uniforms: Why We Are What We Wear.* **Boston: Houghton Mifflin, 2002.**
Uniforms both include and exclude. Fussell, an academic and a very good writer, here focuses with keen cultural insight, sharp anecdotes, and history on the question of why we wear regulated clothing.

Gavenas, Mary Lisa. *The Fairchild Encyclopedia of Menswear.* **New York: Fairchild Publications, 2008.**
A must-have reference book. Entries are generally short and to the point, many with moderately meaningful illustrations and an adequate bibliography.

Girtin, Thomas. *Makers of Distinction: Suppliers to the Town and Country Gentleman.* **London: Harvill, 1959.**
One of the few true classics of the genre, *Makers* charmingly describes a bygone world in which an English gentleman had everything made for him, with the possible exception of underwear and raincoat. A beautifully written tribute to Old World craftsmanship. A charming, sympathetic glimpse into the great age of sartorial artisans.

Hollander, Anne. *Sex and Suits: The Evolution of Modern Dress.* **New York: Knopf, 1994.**
Hollander is an art historian who is able to see a great deal more in a portrait than most of us can. Here she makes the provocative argument that the men's suit is the most modern and sensible of garments by comparing and contrasting it with women's clothing since the eighteenth century.

Kuchta, David. *The Three-Piece Suit and Modern Masculinity: England, 1550–1850.* **Berkeley: University of California Press, 2002.**
I'm assuming that this was once a doctoral dissertation, but never mind. It's the most convincingly thorough argument of how the suit developed in England between the sixteenth and nineteenth centuries. Solid and fascinating social history at its best.

Martin, Richard, and Harold Koda. *Jocks and Nerds: Men's Style in the Twentieth Century.* **New York: Rizzoli, 1989.**
A heavily illustrated consideration of how men have dressed in the twentieth century by genre: worker, rebel, dandy, businessman—you get the idea. Some of these categories seem forced, of course, because modern men's lives and wardrobes have more and more tended to overlap when it comes to genres of dress. It is nevertheless a good general read.

McNeil, Peter, and Vicki Karaminas, eds. *The Men's Fashion Reader.* **Oxford: Berg, 2009.**
Arguably the best single volume on the key writings about men's fashions, edited by well-known scholars in the field. Sections include the history and evolution of menswear, discussions of masculinity and sexuality, subcultures, design, and modes of consumerism. And a very useful bibliography.

Moers, Ellen. *The Dandy: Brummell to Beerbohm*. London: Secker & Warburg, 1960.
The classic, primary study of the subject to which all others are obliged. While other writers have now taken the subject further and in different directions, this is still the best discussion of dandyism in nineteenth-century England and France as you'll likely find.

Perrot, Philippe. *Fashioning the Bourgeoisie: A History of Clothing in the Nineteenth Century*. Princeton, NJ: Princeton University Press, 1994.
Up-to-the-eyebrows annotated and scholarly, yet stimulatingly readable and beautifully written social history. One of the first to attempt to explain a culture's sociology through its choice of clothing.

Roetzel, Bernhard. *Gentleman: A Timeless Guide to Fashion*. Potsdam: Ullmann, 2010.
A handsomely illustrated survey of the gentleman's wardrobe from grooming the beard to shodding the feet, and everything in between. With a useful essay on looking after the wardrobe, a glossary, and a bibliography.

Schoeffler, O. E., and William Gale. *Esquire's Encyclopedia of 20th Century Men's Fashions*. New York: McGraw-Hill, 1973.
Published over forty years ago now, this hefty tome was considered essential and is now something of a collector's pride. A good popular history in encyclopedic form, particularly of the 1930s through '60s periods. Someone should do a revised edition and bring it up to date. Or even just reprint the original.

Shannon, Brent Alan. *The Cut of His Coat: Men, Dress, and Consumer Culture in Britain, 1860–1914*. Athens: Ohio University Press, 2006.
This perfect academic follow-up to the Kuchta study takes the subject of the masculine wardrobe from 1860 to the First World War. Folded in is the social history of consumerism during the period. Exhaustive bibliography.

Sherwood, James. *The London Cut: Savile Row Bespoke Tailoring.* **Milan: Marsilio, 2007.**
A compendium and analysis of Savile Row today by an expert on the subject. Contains a detailed, close, and meticulous discussion of the firms today, including the history, house style, and customers. Should be considered the bible on the subject.

Tortora, Phyllis G., and Robert S. Merkel. *Fairchild's Dictionary of Textiles.* **New York: Fairchild Publications, 1996.**
Considered the standard reference work in the field, a true dictionary of the subject, methodical and approachable by the novice as well as the expert. Intelligently cross-referenced.

Walker, Richard. *Savile Row: An Illustrated History.* **New York: Rizzoli, 1988.**
A fine introduction to the history of the world's most famous enclave of bespoke tailors and their customers from the eighteenth through the twentieth centuries. Well illustrated, and with a useful glossary of professional and slang terms.

NOTES

INTRODUCTION

x   **most communication is nonverbal:** In fact, "nonverbal behavior is the most crucial aspect of communication" (Blake, "How Much of Communication Is Really Nonverbal?," The Nonverbal Group, August 2011, http://www.nonverbalgroup.com/2011/08/how-much-of -communication-is-really-nonverbal).

xii   **"self-confident capitalist class":** David Kuchta, *The Three-Piece Suit and Modern Masculinity: England, 1550–1850* (Berkeley: University of California Press, 2002), 104.

xiv   **"shunned all external peculiarity":** Captain Jesse, *Beau Brummell*, (London: Grolier Society, 1905), vol. 1, 55.

CHAPTER 1

3   **cravats were advertised:** Doriece Colle, *Collars, Stocks, Cravats: A History and Costume Dating Guide to Civilian Men's Neckpieces: 1655–1900* (Emmaus, PA: Rodale, 1972), 6.

5   **biography of the Beau:** Ian Kelly, *Beau Brummell: The Ultimate Man of Style* (New York: Free Press, 2006), 98–99.

5   **"gave subtle expression":** Ibid., 100.

5   **"Oh, sir, those are our failures":** Quoted in Captain Jesse, *Beau Brummell* (London: Grolier Society, 1905), vol. 1, 56.

CHAPTER 2

15   **In the late 1940s the Lucchese Boot Company:** Sharon DeLano and David Rieff, *Texas Boots* (New York: Penguin, 1981), 104–106.

16   **Nathan Clark, a son of the founder:** Mark Palmer, "The Boots That Built an Empire," *Daily Mail* (London), July 1, 2011.

17   **The story is that he loved:** "L. L. Bean, Inc.," *International Directory of Company Histories,* 1995, http://www.encyclopedia.com/doc/1G2–2841400135.html.

CHAPTER 3

20   **two distinct models:** See François Chaille, *The Book of Ties* (Paris: Flammarion, 1994), 109ff., and Alan Flusser, *Dressing the Man* (New York: HarperCollins, 2002), 160–164, for a fuller discussion of these two bow tie styles.

22   **"Whatever style may have been adopted":** H. Le Blanc, *The Art of Tying the Cravat: Demonstrated in Sixteen Lessons,* 3rd ed. (1828; repr., Countess Mara, n.d.), 24–25.

CHAPTER 4

24   **"People took each other's appearances":** Richard Sennett, *The Fall of Public Man* (New York: Norton, 1974), 161.

CHAPTER 5

35   **"When I lately stood":** *Scintillations from the Prose Works of Heinrich Heine,* translated by Simon Adler Stern (New York: Henry Holt, 1873), 94.

37   **"There is hardly anything":** The quotation is frequently attributed to John Ruskin, a nineteenth-century British art critical and social critic. According to George P. Landow, a noted Ruskin scholar, there is no evidence that it can be found in any of Ruskin's works (George P. Landow, "A Ruskin Quotation?," *The Victorian Web: Literature, History & Culture in the Age of Victoria,* July 27, 2007, www.victorianweb.org/authors/ruskin/quotation.html).

CHAPTER 6

41   **Nevada tailor named Jacob Davis:** The story about Davis and Levi Strauss is from "Levi Strauss and Jacob Davis Receive Patent for Blue Jeans," History.com, May 20, 2009, http://www.history.com/this-day-in-history/levi-strauss-and-jacob-davis-receive-patent-for-blue-jeans.

41   **He and Levi took out a joint US patent:** Jacob Davis and Levi Strauss & Co. Improvement in Fastening Pocket-Openings. US Patent 139, 121 A, filed August 9, 1872, and issued May 20, 1873.

CHAPTER 7

48   **"This morning," he recalled:** Robert Latham and William Matthews, editors, *The Diary of Samuel Pepys* (Berkeley: University of California Press, 1979), 2:130.

CHAPTER 8

52   **rooms with old worn carpets:** Mark Hampton, *On Decorating* (New York: Random House, 1989), 133.

52   **"each stratum of taste:** E. F. Benson, *As We Are: A Modern Revue* (London: Hogarth, 1985), 5.

53   **In calling upon gentlemen:** David Kuchta, *The Three-Piece Suit and Modern Masculinity: England, 1550–1850* (Berkeley: University of California Press, 2002), 12–13.

56   **"engaging agglomeration of different styles":** See Vita Sackville-West's charming little book, *English Country Houses* (London: Prion, 1996), 24.

CHAPTER 9

57   **According to fashion reporter Guy Trebay:** Guy Trebay, "For Tuxedos, Blue Is the New Black," *New York Times,* May 21, 2014, www.nytimes.com/2014/05/22/fashion/for-tuxedos-blue-is-the-new-black.html.

59   **John Harvey notes that Chinese emperors:** John Harvey, *Men in Black* (Chicago: University of Chicago Press, 1995), 41–70.

63   **As he explained in his memoir:** H.R.H. the Duke of Windsor, *Windsor Revisited* (Boston: Houghton Mifflin, 1960), 158.

70   **"Not knowing the form":** Cole Lesley, *Remembered Laughter: The Life of Noel Coward* (New York: Knopf, 1976), 43.

CHAPTER 10

73   **so-called bridge frames:** For a fuller definition of this term, see Femke Van Eijk, *Spectacles and Sunglasses* (Amsterdam: Pepin, 2005), 22.

73   **By 1930 celluloid:** These historical details are from Van Eijk, *Spectacles and Sunglasses.*

CHAPTER 11

82 **Reading the various histories and diaries:** The most readable histories are Christopher Hibbert's two-volume biography of George IV and Carolly Erickson's *Our Tempestuous Day: A History of Regency England*; the most vivid personal account is arguably courtesan Harriet Wilson's memoirs; the classic portrait of the period remains T. H. White's *The Age of Scandal.*

83 **"Cleanliness and order are not matters":** Benjamin Disraeli, "Speech at Aylesbury, Royal and Central Bucks Agricultural Association, September 21, 1865," in *Wit and Wisdom of Benjamin Disraeli, Earl of Beaconsfield.* (London: Longmans, Green, 1886), 111.

CHAPTER 12

90 **He reports that Scipio:** Richard A. Gabriel, *Scipio Africanus: Rome's Greatest General* (Washington, DC: Potomac Books, 2008), 3.

91 **The safety razor was first patented:** Mary Bellis, "History of Razors and Shaving," About.com, http://inventors.about.com/library/inventors /blrazor.htm, accessed March 25, 2015.

CHAPTER 13

98 **the Creator had made Italy:** Mark Twain, *The Innocents Abroad* (London: New American Library, 1966), 215.

100 **"The earliest mention specifically of a tailor":** Carole Collier Frick, *Dressing Renaissance Florence: Families, Fortunes, and Fine Clothing* (Baltimore: Johns Hopkins University Press, 2002), 13.

102 **It is, incidentally, one of the reasons:** Luigi Barzini, *The Italians* (New York: Atheneum, 1964), 90.

102 **"I never heard from human lips":** Nathaniel Hawthorne, *Passages from the French and Italian Notebooks* (Boston: James R. Osgood and Company, 1876), 45.

103 **"Italia, oh, Italia!:** Lord Byron, "Childe Harold's Pilgrimage," Canto 4, Stanza 42, ll. 1–2, in *Lord Byron: The Major Works* (Oxford: Oxford University Press, 2008).

CHAPTER 14

117 **My friend Christian Chensvold:** Conversation with the author. See Christian Chensvold's blog *Ivy Style* for his various writings on this point.

CHAPTER 16

129 **"the clearest and most elegant medium":** François duc de La Rochefoucauld, *Maxims*, translated by L. W. Tancock (London: Penguin, 1959), 12.

CHAPTER 17

135 **"more like some kind of foreign tenor":** Lytton Strachey, *Queen Victoria* (New York: Harcourt, Brace, 1921), Chapter 4, gutenberg .org/files/1265/1265-h/1265-h.htm.

136 **fashion is echo:** Cornel West, "What Is Style?" YouTube video, 3:20, *Prepidemic Magazine*, May 23, 2010, youtube.com/watch?v=4SHc JPMvmzU.

CHAPTER 18

138 **"True art is what does not:** Baldesar Castiglione, *The Book of the Courtier*, translated by George Bull (London: Penguin, 1986), 67.

CHAPTER 19

144 **Aesthetic judgment, as Susan Sontag noted:** See Susan Sontag, *As Consciousness Is Harnessed to Flesh: Journals & Notebooks (1964–1980)* (New York: Picador, 2013).

146 **"In the 1830s the male costume":** Richard Sennett, *The Fall of Public Man* (New York: Norton, 1976), 163.

147 **in 1900, John Brooks:** *Encyclopedia of Clothing and Fashion*, ed. Valerie Steele (Farmington Hills, MI: Charles Scribner's Sons, 2005), 1:197.

148 **One night at Nick's:** Charles Fountain, *Another Man's Poison: The Life and Writing of Columnist George Frazier* (Chester, CT: Globe Pequot, 1984), 41.

154 **"triangular sector formed":** Alan Flusser, *Dressing the Man* (New York: HarperCollins, 2002), 123.

CHAPTER 20

162 **"His suit was of a striped":** Theodore Dreiser, *Sister Carrie* (New York: Library of America, 1987), 5.

CHAPTER 21

166 **shortened trousers were worn:** W. Y. Carman, *A Dictionary of Military Uniform* (New York: Charles Scribner's Sons, 1977), 119.

166 **the most popular sport of '30s Britain:** Robert Graves and Alan Hodge, *The Long Weekend: A Social History of Great Britain 1918–1939* (New York: Norton, 1963), 265–280.

168 **"seemed anxious to make up":** O. E. Schoeffler and William Gale, editors, *Esquire's Encyclopedia of 20th Century Men's Fashions* (New York: McGraw-Hill, 1973), 85.

168 **"in everything from solid colors":** Schoeffler and Gale, *Esquire's Encyclopedia*, 85.

CHAPTER 22

172 **"There is no longer a public self":** Jill Lepore, "The Prism," *New Yorker*, June 24, 2013, 32–36.

172 **Voltaire credited with greatly contributing:** See François duc de La Rochefoucauld, *Maxims*, translated by L. W. Tancock (London: Penguin, 1959).

172 **letters to his son illuminate:** See Lord Chesterfield, *Letters*, edited by David Roberts (Oxford: Oxford University Press, 1992).

172 **"I have discovered a universal rule":** Baldesar Castiglione, *The Book of the Courtier*, translated by George Bull (London: Penguin, 1986), 67.

173 **"A man who performs well:** Castiglione, *The Book of the Courtier*, 70.

173 **Stephen Potter:** *The Theory and Practice of Gamesmanship or The Art of Winning Games Without Actually Cheating* (New York: BN Publications, 2008).

174 **A sweete disorder in the dresse:** Robert Herrick, "Delight in Disorder," in *The Norton Anthology of English Literature*, vol. 1, edited by M. H. Abrams (New York: Norton, 1968), 944.

177 **My neckcloth, of course:** Quoted in Ian Kelly, *Beau Brummell: The Ultimate Man of Style* (New York: Free Press, 2006), 98.

179 **True Ease . . . comes from Art:** Alexander Pope, "An Essay on Criticism," ll. 362–363, in *The Poems of Alexander Pope*, edited by John Butt (New Haven, CT: Yale University Press, 1963).

CHAPTER 23

181 **"The King hath yesterday in council":** *The Diary of Samuel Pepys, Vol. 7, 1666,* edited by Robert Latham and William Matthews, (Berkeley: University of California Press, 1974), 315.

182 **This day the King begins:** *Diary of Samuel Pepys,* 324.

182 **"Being loose and comfortable":** C. Willett Cunnington and Phillis Cunnington, *Handbook of English Costume in the Nineteenth Century* (Boston: Plays, Inc., 1970), 231.

183 **"advances in technology:** Anne Hollander, *Sex and Suits* (New York: Knopf, 1994), 4–5.

CHAPTER 24

190 **"I have found":** "Mark Twain in White Amuses Congressmen, Advocates New Copyright Law and Dress Reform," *New York Times*, December 8, 1906, http://www.twainquotes.com/19061208.html.

191 **"no even halfway proper gentleman":** Brian Abel Ragen, *Tom Wolfe: A Critical Companion* (Westport, CT: Greenwood Press, 2002), 12.

191 **"the spread of linen":** Daniel Roche, *The Culture of Clothing: Dress and Fashion in the Ancien Regime* (Cambridge: Cambridge University Press, 1994), 156.

192 **he discovered that forty-two:** This story is quoted by Roche from Rousseau's *Les Confessions*; the incident had occurred sometime around 1750.

192 **"very fine linen, plenty of it":** Ian Kelly, *Beau Brummell: The Ultimate Man of Style* (New York: Free Press, 2006), 95.

CHAPTER 25

204 **social history of Great Britain between the wars:** Robert Graves and Alan Hodge, *The Long Weekend: A Social History of Great Britain 1918–1939* (New York: Norton, 1963).

205 **"Everyone was wearing":** Evelyn Waugh, *The Diaries of Evelyn Waugh* (Boston: Little, Brown, 1976), 188.

206 **"the original anything goes joint":** Steven Watson, *The Birth of the Beat Generation: Visionaries, Rebels, and Hipsters 1944–1960* (New York: Pantheon, 1995), 243.

CHAPTER 26

210 **He cites the tailcoat:** James Laver, *The Concise History of Costume and Fashion* (New York: Abrams, 1969), 256–259.

212 **"India rubber cloth":** *The Encyclopedia of Clothing and Fashion*, edited by Valerie Steele (Farmington Hills, MI: Charles Scribner's Sons, 2005), 3:79.

INDEX

G. Bruce Boyer is a renowned expert on menswear and men's fashion. He has authored, co-authored, and contributed to numerous books on fashion, and his feature articles have appeared in *Esquire*, *Harper's Bazaar*, *Forbes*, the *New York Times*, the *New Yorker*, *Departures*, and the *Rake*, among other national and international magazines. Boyer has also co-curated several fashion exhibitions at The Museum at the Fashion Institute of Technology. He lives in Bethlehem, Pennsylvania.